10/04

28.70

NATIONS **IN TRANSITION**

CHINA

New and future titles in the
Nations in Transition series include:

- India
- Indonesia
- Iran
- Ireland
- North Korea
- Pakistan
- Russia
- South Korea
- Vietnam

NATIONS **IN TRANSITION**

CHINA

by Tony Zurlo

San Diego • Detroit • New York • San Francisco • Cleveland
New Haven, Conn. • Waterville, Maine • London • Munich

For more information, contact
Greenhaven Press
27500 Drake Rd.
Farmington Hills, MI 48331-3535
Or you can visit our Internet site at http://www.gale.com

LIBRARY OF CONGRESS CATALOGING-IN-PUBLICATION DATA

Zurlo, Tony, 1941–
China / by Tony Zurlo.
p. cm. — (Nations in transition)
Includes bibliographical references (p.).and index
Contents: A nation defined by change—Culture—The People's Republic of China.
Summary: Discusses the history, conflict, people, and changes through modern day China.
ISBN 0-7377-1204-X (hardback : alk. paper)
1. China—Juvenile literature. [1. China] I. Title. II. Series.
2003
—dc21

Printed in the United States of America

Contents

Foreword

In 1986 Soviet general secretary Mikhail Gorbachev initiated his plan to reform the economic, political, and social structure of the Soviet Union. Nearly three-quarters of a century of Communist ideology was dismantled in the next five years. As the totalitarian regime relaxed its rule and opened itself up to the West, the Soviet peoples clamored for more freedoms. Hard-line Communists resisted Gorbachev's lead, but glasnost, or "openness," could not be stopped with the will of the common people behind it.

In 1991 the changing USSR held its first multicandidate elections. The reform-minded Boris Yeltsin, a supporter of Gorbachev, became the first popularly elected president of the Russian Republic in Soviet history. Under Yeltsin's leadership, the old Communist policies soon all but disintegrated, as did the Soviet Union itself. The Union of Soviet Socialist Republics broke apart into fifteen independent entities. The former republics reformed into a more democratic union now referred to as the Commonwealth of Independent States. Russia remained the nominal figurehead of the commonwealth, but it no longer dictated the future of the other independent states.

By the new millennium, Russia and the other commonwealth states still faced crises. The new states were all in transition from decades of totalitarian rule to the postglasnost era of unprecedented and untested democratic reforms. Revamping the Soviet economy may have opened up new opportunities in private ownership of property and business, but it did not bring overnight prosperity to the former republics. Common necessities such as food still remain in short supply in many regions. And while new governments seek to stabilize their authority, crime rates have escalated throughout the former Soviet Union. Still, the people are confident that their newfound freedoms—freedom of speech and assembly, freedom of religion, and even the right of workers to strike—will ultimately better their lives. The process of change will take time and the people are willing to see their respective states through the challenges of this transitional period in Soviet history.

The collapse and rebuilding of the former Soviet Union provides perhaps the best example of a contemporary "nation in transition," the focus of this Greenhaven Press series. However, other nations that fall under the series rubric have faced a host of unique and varied cultural shifts. India, for instance, is a stable, guiding force in Asia, yet it remains a nation in transition more than fifty years after winning independence from Great Britain. The entire infrastructure of the Indian subcontinent still bears the marking of its colonial past: In a land of eighteen official spoken languages, for example, English remains the voice of politics and education. India is still coming to grips with its colonial legacy while forging its place as a strong player in Asian and world affairs.

North Korea's place in Greenhaven's Nations in Transition series is based on major recent political developments. After decades of antagonism between its Communist government and the democratic leadership of South Korea, tensions seemed to ease in the late 1990s. Even under the shadow of the North's developing nuclear capabilities, the presidents of both North and South Korea met in 2000 to propose plans for possible reunification of the two estranged nations. And though it is one of the three remaining bastions of communism in the world, North Korea is choosing not to remain an isolated relic of the Cold War. While it has not earned the trust of the United States and many of its Western allies, North Korea has begun to reach out to its Asian neighbors to encourage trade and cultural exchanges.

These three countries exemplify the types of changes and challenges that qualify them as subjects of study in the Greenhaven Nations in Transition series. The series examines specific nations to disclose the major social, political, economic, and cultural shifts that have caused massive change and in many cases, brought about regional and/or worldwide shifts in power. Detailed maps, inserts, and pictures help flesh out the people, places, and events that define the country's transitional period. Furthermore, a comprehensive bibliography points readers to other sources that will deepen their understanding of the nation's complex past and contemporary struggles. With these tools, students and casual readers trace both past history and future challenges of these important nations.

Introduction

A Long Journey

When Mao Zedong proclaimed the People's Republic of China in 1949, the nation entered a period of peace for the first time in almost a century. Mao declared that China was ready to stand proudly alongside other independent nations. But predictable and permanent economic and political advancement was obstructed by Mao's oppressive ideology. Another twenty-six years passed before the pragmatic leadership of Deng Xiaoping unleashed the talents of a billion people to modernize China's economy.

China's transition from a poverty-stricken nation barely able to feed itself to a country boasting the seventh-largest economy in the world has been dramatic. During the last two decades of the twentieth century, the Chinese people threw aside the fears and troubles of the Mao era and dedicated themselves to the pursuit of economic prosperity. China enters the twenty-first century with high hopes of becoming one of the major economic forces in the world in two or three generations. At the incredible pace that the economy has grown for more than two decades—between 7 and 10 percent annually—China seems to be accelerating through its journey to wealth faster than anyone could have predicted.

Pragmatic Economic Reform

Both Deng Xiaoping and his successor, Jiang Zemin, established a legacy of pragmatism in governing the country during the last part of the twentieth century. They introduced a market-driven economy, closed down thousands of unprofitable state-owned enterprises, and encouraged private businesses to open. As a result of these economic reforms, the vast majority of Chinese live more comfortably today than ever before in history.

Chinese officials continue to face challenges, however. For one, China has yet to narrow the huge rural-urban income gap.

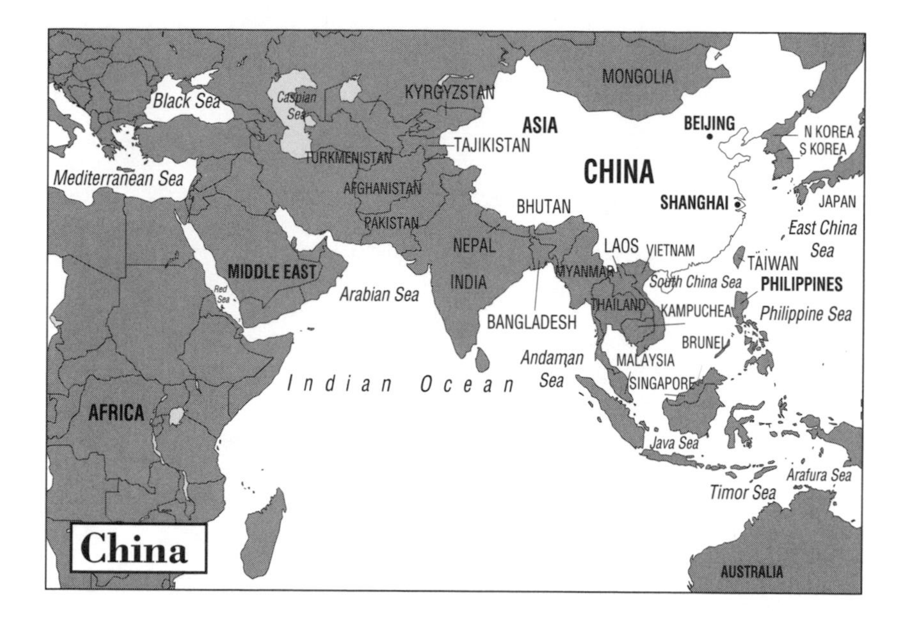

China

As a result, there is an enormous migration of peasants into cities numbering approximately 300 million. They add to an increasing urban unemployment rate that has officially reached more than 5 percent. Private enterprise cannot yet absorb the tens of millions of workers who lose their jobs when state-owned enterprises shut down. In addition, China's industrial growth and expanding energy use has brought China the most serious pollution problem in the world.

China's efforts at addressing these problems have not gone unnoticed. The 2001 Human Development Report of the United Nations Development Programme assesses 162 countries for how well their citizens compare in "longevity, educational attainment and ability to buy basic goods and services." China jumped from ninety-ninth on the list in 2000 to eighty-seventh in 2001. The report names China as one of the few nations "on track to meet the goal of halving poverty by 2015."[1]

China's Future

China's future is in the hands of a young generation that knows little about China's past struggles. Members of this generation take for granted the opportunities to open up private businesses, to invest in the stock market, and to surf the Internet for up-to-

The freedom and opportunity the younger generation of Chinese enjoys today is unprecedented and makes it difficult for them to relate to the struggles of their elders.

date world and national news. Those people under forty years of age are at ease with Western ideas and culture.

Younger Chinese enjoy far more freedoms than the Chinese people have had at any time since the Communists took power. And the rapid expansion of technology in communications is knocking down government obstructions. The ruling Communist Party understands the urgency of adapting to changing times and conditions. To maintain its control of the country, the party has not only begun to incorporate capitalist ideas but it is also inviting capitalists to become members. In addition, the party has allowed competitive elections in villages and towns across China. There are even talks among high-level government advisers of experimenting with provincial and national elections.

Much of China's incentive to become a more open society is driven by entry into the World Trade Organization (WTO). As a member, China expects long-term economic growth. But just as important, membership in the WTO requires China to speed up its economic and political reforms. Authorities are already revising thousands of laws so they can protect private business rights. With this grassroots transformation of the business culture comes pressure for more political reform. And most experts believe the Communist Party will have to change its authoritarian ways to survive.

The response of China's leaders to the challenges they face is of more than passing interest to the world at large. With a population of more than a billion, China represents an unprecedented opportunity to anyone with a product to sell. At the same time, such a large population presents a potential threat to stability in the region if the nation's leaders are unable to deliver on their promises. How China came to be at this crossroad is a fascinating story.

Mao Zedong Unifies the Middle Kingdom

1

An ancient Chinese adage advises that "A journey of a thousand miles begins with a single step." In 1912, China took that first step out of a world in which corrupt imperial officials conspired with foreign powers to bleed the people dry. Revolutionaries overthrew the emperor in hopes of overhauling their archaic economic and political systems so that China would become a world power, able to compete successfully with the West and Japan.

In the latter half of the nineteenth century, Western powers referred to China as "the Sick Man of Asia." With a population larger than all the other east Asian nations combined, China entered the twentieth century a crippled, hopelessly archaic society. The weak emperors of the Qing dynasty had allowed the powerful European nations to take over large portions of coastal territory from which to conduct trade. In addition, most efforts to modernize China were thwarted by self-serving officials who were concerned about preserving their positions rather than reforming the feudal system under which a small number of landlords grew rich from the labor of landless peasants.

The major problem in China was that peasants, who made up 90 percent of the population, were trapped in a cycle of endless fieldwork. Often, much of their harvest went to local officials and landlords in payment of taxes, rent, and interest on loans. Of those peasants who did own land, some had to sell part of their holdings to pay debts, and even those who had not been forced to sell land still normally owned less than three acres, barely enough to allow them to feed themselves and make their payments. Tens of millions of homeless and landless peasants had to rent land from landlords in return for as much as 50 to 70 percent of their harvests.

As the twentieth century approached, China was so far behind the Western countries and Japan in terms of economic and military power that some Chinese believed their nation would lose its independence and become divided up into colonies ruled by European nations and Japan. These individuals argued strongly that the only way China could retain its sovereignty was to adopt Western ideas for running the country. Officials advising the emperor, however, argued that Chinese culture was superior to the ways of foreigners. Historian Frederic Wakeman

Peasants were often indebted to local officials and landlords, trapping them in a cycle of poverty and labor.

Sun Yatsen's Three Principles of the People helped push China to change.

Jr. explains their viewpoint, which was based in Confucian philosophy: "Better men, not laws, would save the empire; moral improvement, not institutional tinkering, would guarantee good government. . . . It was impossible to graft one culture's products on another society."[2]

Sun Yatsen's Three Principles

Many Chinese, however, insisted that China could be saved only by abolishing the Confucian social order. The most prominent spokesman for such radical change between 1885 and 1925 was Sun Yatsen. Sun called his program the Three Principles of the People. The first of these principles was nationalism. Chinese patriotism, Sun claimed, would provide the incentive to eliminate Western domination of China. His second principle was democracy, which involved overthrowing the corrupt monarchy and replacing it with an elected government. Sun's third goal was to adopt a form of socialism for the economy, under which land would be redistributed, giving all people a chance to improve their standard of living by keeping a greater share of what they grew.

Sun's efforts were made easier by dissatisfaction in China's military with the emperor's leadership. The nation had suffered humiliating defeats in several conflicts with Japan and European nations, and most Chinese blamed their emperor for this turn of events. Many military officers plotted rebellion.

By 1911 revolts against the Qing emperor Pu yi were flaring up continuously in central and southern China both among workers and young military men. China's troubles came to a head in the summer of 1911, when demonstrations broke out against a government plan to finance with foreign loans the building of a railroad line connecting the southern cities of Guangzhou and Chengdu. Private Chinese investors had already committed their own money to the project, so they took advantage of popular antiforeign sentiment to foment opposition to the government itself. On October 11 a large army unit in Wuhan mutinied and convinced their superior officers to declare Hubei province independent from the central government in Beijing. Within weeks, several other provincial military leaders followed Hubei's lead.

An Unfinished Revolution

Within two months all of China's provinces had declared their independence from the empire, and they called on Sun Yatsen to serve as the first president of a new nation called the Chinese Republic. To convince the Qing officials to surrender power peacefully, Sun called in Yuan Shikai, who had close ties with the dynasty. Yuan convinced the emperor and his advisers to give up their claim to rule China.

Sun backed Yuan as the Chinese Republic's president, but within a year Yuan had betrayed the ideals of the revolution and revived authoritarian rule. In 1915 Yuan planned his own installation as emperor. However, opposition was so widespread and severe that he gave up that plan. Meanwhile, the various warlords who controlled various pieces of Chinese territory paid little attention to the central government. China was essentially divided up into many semi-independent states.

Opposition to Yuan's shaky rule spread in 1915, when word leaked out that Yuan was considering giving in to Japan's Twenty-one Demands, a document in which Japan requested special privileges that would place major areas of eastern China under Japanese control. Yuan backed down after students and intellectuals all across China protested; however, Japan already occupied much of the Shandong Peninsula in eastern China and refused to leave.

The Guomindang Party

Yuan became ill and died in 1916, and China entered an even more unstable period of civil conflict. While competing warlords fought for power, two rival governments claimed to be the legitimate successors of the 1911 revolution. The northern government in Beijing was opposed by a series of governments in southern China, often led by Sun Yatsen's Guomindang Party (GMD). Moreover, neither government had the military power to exert meaningful authority, and both depended on various warlords for support.

Sun sought financial assistance for his nation, but the United States and a number of European nations turned him down. Russia, however, did provide aid. Russian advisers also restructured the GMD along the lines of the Russian Communist Party and insisted that Communists be allowed to join the GMD to strengthen the party's opposition to the warlords. Some of Sun's most promising followers were sent to Russia for training.

Mao Zedong helped form the Chinese Communist Party in 1921.

Enter Mao Zedong

While Sun was trying to unify the nation, another force in Chinese politics, the New Culture Movement, was growing in strength among many Chinese intellectuals. The supporters of this movement, including a young nationalist named Mao Zedong, argued for a cultural revolution that would eliminate traditional Chinese values and substitute Western science and social theory—including communism.

The supporters of the New Culture Movement and others who called for profound changes in China had reason for hope. World War I had ended with the defeat of Germany, which had occupied Shandong province since 1897, and China expected that territory would be returned. However, the 1919 Treaty of Versailles, which officially ended World War I, handed over German holdings to Japan. In response, protest demonstrations broke out in Beijing and spread across China.

The dissatisfaction with the terms of the Treaty of Versailles quickly evolved into a general call for sweeping change within China. On May 4, 1919, intellectuals, students, and workers nationwide joined in demonstrations that became a rallying cry for reform. What soon came to be called the May Fourth Movement rallied educated Chinese to demand economic, social, and political reform in China.

The Communist Party

To many Chinese, it was apparent that poverty was at the heart of their nation's troubles. Many leaders of the May Fourth and New Culture Movements saw in socialism and communism a way to lead China out of its extreme poverty. In 1920 and 1921, the Russian-sponsored Communist International (Comintern) sent representatives to China to encourage revolution against the remaining Western powers that enjoyed special privileges there.

In July 1921 twelve men (including Mao Zedong) gathered secretly in Shanghai and founded the Chinese Communist Party (CCP) under the guidance of the Comintern. They declared loyalty to the Leninist-Marxist principle of class struggle.

The Peasant Revolution

Mao, who quickly became a dominant force in the CCP, concluded that if the Communists were to succeed in their revolution, they would need to enlist the aid of the nation's peasants. Peasants in Mao's home province of Hunan had already begun fighting landlords' high rents and forming unions, and in 1925 Mao set out to tour Hunan and recruit members for the new party. Historian Ross Terrill writes that, because of Mao's efforts, "by the end of 1926, . . . half of Hunan's 75 counties had peasant unions. Two million peasants belonged."[3] Based on this

Young Rebel

As China entered the twentieth century, in the southern Chinese mountain village of Shaoshan a young boy named Mao Zedong was receiving a traditional Confucian education. Although he was trained to keep financial records for his father, who was a rich peasant and grain merchant, Mao rebelled at an early age. In his book *Mao: A Biography*, Ross Terrill explains that one day in class the ten-year-old Mao refused to stand when his Confucian teacher called on him. Mao challenged, "If you can hear me well while I sit down, why should I stand up to recite?" The teacher ordered Mao to kneel before him, but instead, Mao "dragged his stool to the teacher's desk and sat looking at him in calm defiance. The enraged teacher pulled at Zedong to raise him upright. Zedong writhed free and marched out of the school. Like the rebels in the *Story of the Marshes*, he took refuge in the hills." He stayed away for three days before returning. Mao says that after the incident his "father was slightly more considerate and the teacher was more inclined to moderation. The result of my act of protest impressed me very much. It was a successful 'strike.'"

experience, Mao published an article in which he set out his plan for revolution.

In the article Mao pointed out that China's peasants were the worst victims of oppression. Mao shifted the emphasis of Communist doctrine away from Karl Marx's contention that urban, industrial workers would be the vehicle for Communist revolutions around the world. Terrill writes, "It was a startling conclusion. The revolution would stand or fall with the peasants. . . . With this article Karl Marx sank into the rice paddies of Asia."[4] In early 1927 Mao once again toured counties in Hunan. In his report on this tour, Mao claimed that peasant union membership had ballooned to 5 million. According to Terrill, Mao found "landlords being paraded in tall paper hats by crowds beating gongs. The most hated types he found already locked up . . . [many for] hoarding grain to keep the price up."[5]

The Guomindang-Communist Split

China's Communists soon found themselves with an opponent. When Sun Yatsen died in 1925, the GMD's military leader,

Chiang Kaishek, took over as head of the party. After Chiang subdued China's powerful southern warlords, he turned his attention to what he saw as the growing threat of the CCP.

Communists had seized control of the government in the Chinese port city of Shanghai, and Chiang sent his troops to attack. Tens of thousands of Communist soldiers were killed during the fighting that followed. Eventually, disorganized and disillusioned, most of the remaining CCP members—about seven thousand—fled westward into the mountains of the Jiangxi province. The Communists were left in control of what they called the Soviet Republic of China, consisting of a small cluster of counties in south central China.

With little territory under its control and pressed by Chiang Kaishek and his forces, the CCP split into two factions. One group, under Russian-trained leaders, followed a strategy that stressed uprisings by urban workers, military attacks on large urban centers, and radical land redistribution in the countryside.

Chiang Kaishek was the CCP's biggest opponent and it was his main goal to rid China of communism.

Mao and his faction promoted a strategy of peasant uprisings, avoidance of large urban areas, and redistribution of land only when practical.

The National Government Under Chiang Kaishek

Meanwhile, the government under Chiang Kaishek and the Guomindang was recognized by most of the world's nations. Yet to remain in power, Chiang had to find ways to solve three major problems: a chronically sick economy, further invasions by Japanese troops, and agitation by Communists in the countryside. Chiang was convinced that he could not solve the first two problems until he had eradicated communism.

Translating Chinese into English

Until the 1970s the most popular system of transcribing Chinese sounds into English was the Wades-Giles system, but in the 1930s an alternate system of romanization, known as pinyin, came into use as well. Once in power, Chinese Communist officials refined the system, which simplifies the spelling and more accurately connects the sounds of Chinese with the Roman letter. Both systems remain in use outside of China, although pinyin is gaining in popularity.

Some of the more common changes from Wade-Giles to pinyin include the following:

Wade-Giles	Pinyin	Description
Mao Tse-tung	Mao Zedong	Leader of the Communist revolution
Chou En-lai	Zhou Enlai	Popular premier and foreign minister
Teng Hsiao-peng	Deng Xiaoping	China's leader after Mao's death
Canton	Guangzhou	Important port city in southeastern China
Sian	Xi'an	Ancient capital, located in central China
Peking	Beijing	Capital of China
Szechuan	Sichuan	Province in southwestern China
Kuomintang	Guomindang	Nationalist Party, founded by Sun Yatsen and led after his death by Chiang Kaishek

With this goal in mind, Chiang tightened his grip on the nation through the GMD. Beginning with its Executive Committee at the top and extending into every branch of government, the Guomindang ran the country. Chiang's censors controlled China's press, and his police broke up mass meetings of workers, students, and other citizens. GMD officials set agendas for chambers of commerce in the cities and pressured merchants to donate money to support the party. To help enforce his policies, Chiang called on allies among China's organized criminals, especially the Green Gang, who were willing to do his bidding, whether it was legal or not.

Concentrating on the cities, Chiang left rural China alone. In the countryside, warlords stepped up their oppression of the peasants by adding more taxes, increasing rents, and confiscating land from those who could not pay. Historian Immanuel C.Y. Hsu summarizes the peasants' plight under the GMD government during the mid-1930s: "Tenant and semitenant farming comprised 60–90 per cent in South China, and in addition to paying 40–60 per cent of the annual crops as rental, they had to pay for their landlords' regular land tax and surtax as well—the latter varying from 35 per cent to 350 per cent of the former."[6]

Between 1931 and 1934 Chiang conducted four military campaigns against the Communists—which he characterized as "bandit suppression"—all with little success. A fifth campaign, however, carried out in 1934, nearly destroyed his bitter enemy. With nine hundred thousand troops Chiang pressed down on the heart of the Communist force in southern Jiangxi. Under attack, about one hundred thousand Communist soldiers and party members began a retreat west in October 1934.

The Long March

As the Communist troops retreated into the mountains, Mao began challenging the military decisions of those in command. Whenever Mao prevailed in his arguments, the Communist forces were better able to evade Chiang's troops. As a result of his successes, Mao was named head of the Military Council, a position that put him in charge of the retreat. This famous retreat, later referred to as the

Mao, who led the Long March, emerged as the leader of China's Communist movement.

Long March, marked Mao's emergence as the leader of China's Communist movement and the consequent waning of Russia's influence in China's affairs. Ross Terrill notes that "the Chinese Revolution had emerged from under Moscow's shadow."[7]

After deflecting attacks from Chiang's army and various warlords over the course of one year and six thousand miles, Mao led a hardened group of seven to eight thousand Communists into Yanan in the Shaanxi province. During the Long March, Mao urged two lines of strategy: one was land redistribution and village cooperation; the other was combining all of China's energy and forces to drive out the Japanese invaders who had occupied Manchuria in addition to the Shandong province.

Mao's anti-Japanese position made Chiang's attacks on Chinese Communist forces seem unpatriotic by comparison. So compelling was Mao's stance, in fact, that in December 1936 troops that Chiang had stationed in the central Chinese city of Xi'an rebelled against their leader. In what became known as the Xi'an Incident, officers kidnapped Chiang when he visited the city and forced him to agree to a united front with the Communists against the Japanese.

The Anti-Japanese War

The war against the Japanese had largely been confined to the north, but on July 7, 1937, a Japanese patrol on maneuvers asked to enter a small walled town south of Beijing. When the Chinese refused, the Japanese shelled and then occupied the

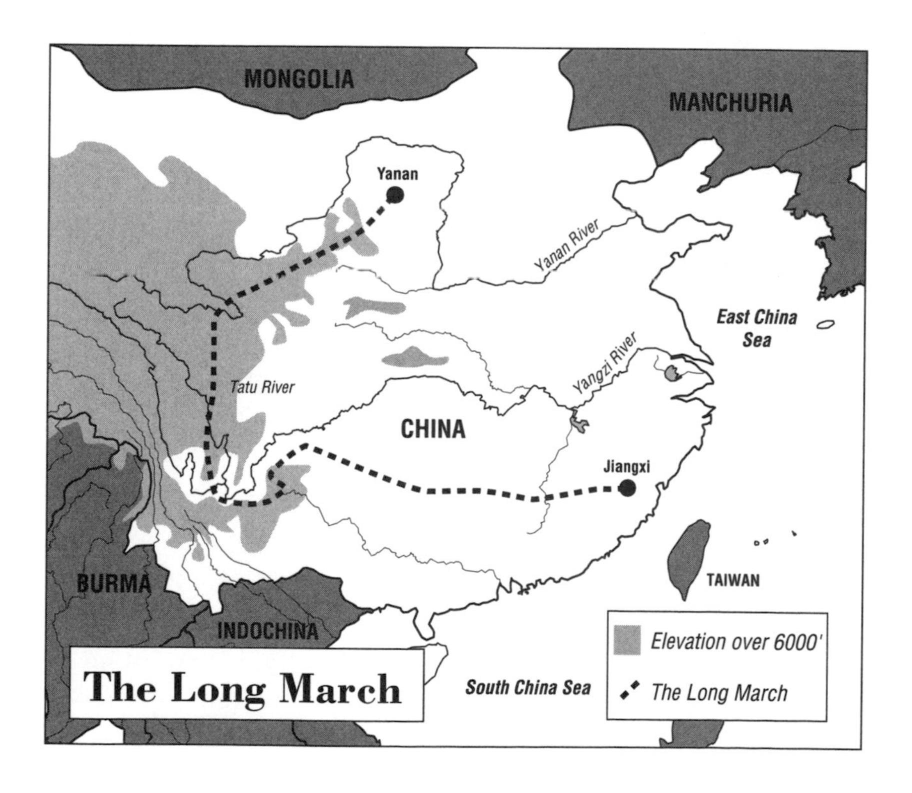

The Long March

Chinese soldiers surrender to Japanese troops during the invasion of Shanghai.

town. Japanese reinforcements poured out of Manchuria in a full-fledged invasion. By July 28 Beijing had surrendered. In August the Japanese began their siege of the port city of Shanghai. After two months of bitter fighting and heavy casualties, Chiang's troops withdrew. The Japanese swiftly took advantage of the opening, capturing Guangzhou, to the south, by October. In December the Japanese overran Nanjing, the location of China's capital. By 1940 Japan occupied or controlled most of the important Chinese cities from Manchuria in the north to the Vietnam border in the south.

The united front agreed upon between the Nationalists and the Communists had a short life. The Communist-led New Fourth Army (NFA) troops were nominally under Chiang's command, and in the fall of 1940, he ordered their withdrawal north of the Yangzi River near Shanghai. In January 1941, as the final five thousand NFA troops prepared to leave, Nationalist troops attacked them. Thousands were killed, and the rest were taken prisoner by the Nationalists. The prisoners were marched to a concentration camp, but only about three hundred survived. The rest had been beaten, shot, or buried alive on the four-hundred-mile-long march.

Communist Wartime Efforts

Ironically, despite their losses the Anti-Japanese War helped the CCP grow tremendously. To the majority of Chinese, Mao and his fellow Communists seemed patriotic. Drawing new members largely from the peasantry, the CCP membership multiplied from forty thousand in 1937 to 1.2 million in 1945. By 1944 the Communists had total or partial control over eighteen "liberated regions" consisting of about three hundred thousand square miles, home to more than 90 million people. The army had grown from fewer than a hundred thousand in 1935 to more than a million regular troops and twice that many peasant militiamen by 1945.

Troops in the Communist army adhered to strict discipline. They were required to memorize and sing daily eight rules for treatment of the peasants. Among other things, these stipulated that soldiers "be honest in all transactions with the peasants" and "pay for articles purchased."[8] This policy contrasted sharply with the Nationalist soldiers' practice of beating the peasants and stealing what they needed. Mao also commanded that his troops help the peasants in their daily work. By their behavior, the Communists almost always gained a strong following from the people.

In the regions where they ruled, the Communists taught peasants to read and write, participate in village government, and take up arms and fight. As journalists Theodore H. White and Annalee Jacoby write, "In Communist areas where the Japanese could not penetrate, the peasants actually lived better during the war than they had before."[9]

Using guerrilla tactics worked out by Mao and his main military commander, Zhu De, Communist soldiers successfully harassed and evaded both Japanese and Nationalist troops. Mao summarized his guerrilla strategy with four slogans: "1. When

Zhou Enlai

Even as a high school student, Zhou Enlai displayed the charm, writing skills, and quick intelligence that would make him one of China's most popular leaders. As a twenty-two-year-old organizer of student protests against China's weak government, Zhou was jailed in January 1920. After his release he spent four years in Europe organizing and training revolutionaries among overseas Chinese. His charismatic personality and good looks opened doors wherever he went, but Zhou never vacillated in his personal honesty and his dedication to building a new, modern China.

Zhou returned to China to work with both the Communist and Guomindang parties to unify China. In early 1927 Zhou organized a workers' takeover of the warlord-controlled Shanghai government. Instead of backing Zhou's forces, Guomindang troops attacked the workers and Communists, killing thousands. Zhou was arrested, but he escaped and fled southward to the city of Wuhan. In July 1927 Zhou barely escaped another bloody campaign by the Guomindang in Wuhan to eliminate the Communists. From that point onward, Zhou worked tirelessly for Communist victory against Chiang Kaishek's Guomindang.

Zhou Enlai

Zhou soon became an unwavering supporter of Mao Zedong's theory of peasant-based revolution. Zhou was at Mao's side throughout the Long March. Whenever Mao needed the skills of a brilliant diplomat and negotiator, he called on Zhou. During World War II Zhou worked with Chiang Kaishek and the American military leaders to plan strategy against the Japanese. After the war, Zhou accompanied Mao in his military campaigns. Together they mapped out the future of the People's Republic of China.

Zhou served as China's premier and the nation's primary contact with foreign nations during the stormy two decades of Mao's rule. But he made his most important contribution to the PRC as a peacemaker between warring factions during the Cultural Revolutions. He prevailed because, unlike the majority of party officials around him, he had no desire for personal power. The enormous outpouring of grief from the Chinese people when Zhou died in 1976 demonstrated how closely they associated Zhou with China itself.

the enemy advances, we retreat! 2. When the enemy halts and encamps, we trouble them! 3. When the enemy seeks to avoid a battle, we attack! 4. When the enemy retreats, we pursue!"[10]

Mao Revives the Communist Movement at Yanan

Gradually, Mao reshaped the CCP to the point that his ideals and desires and those of the party were virtually indistinguishable. During the war Mao remained in Yanan, where he consolidated his position as head of the CCP and directed the Communists' guerrilla campaigns. He also wrote extensively, and so influential were his writings that his core ideas regarding peasant-centered communism were incorporated into the preamble of the CCP constitution in 1945.

Mao, however, discouraged rigid adherence to any doctrine, saying that experience should guide the party. "Theory has not kept pace with revolutionary experience," he told a gathering of a thousand party members in 1942 as part of a campaign to encourage party members to go into the field and learn from working with the peasants and fighting against the Nationalists. In another speech he railed against intellectuals who parroted Marxist-Leninist theories but had little or no practical experience, saying, "If you have not investigated, you have no right to speak."[11]

To Mao, theory had to fit the situation; otherwise, it was worthless rhetoric. Throughout his life Mao's approach was pragmatic, saying of Marxist-Leninist theory, it "has no beauty, nor has it any mystical value. It is only extremely useful."[12]

The Communist Victory of 1949

By late summer 1945 the Japanese had been defeated, but peace had not come to China. Now the Nationalists and the Communists concentrated on battling each other. Many historians argue that Chiang Kaishek should have won the civil war against the Communists, but that his policies alienated the people. He began with vastly superior numbers of troops and equipment and the backing of the United States. However, his government was so corrupt that money was siphoned off at every level of

Standing at the edge of Tiananmen Square on October 1, 1949, Mao declares the victory of the Communist Party and the birth of the People's Republic of China.

government. Taxes mushroomed out of control. Inflation spiraled upward. Land reform, which Chiang had promised during the early 1930s, was abandoned. In fact, very few of Chiang's promised reforms ever materialized.

On the battlefield Chiang held the large cities, but 85 to 90 percent of the people lived in the countryside. By 1948 the Nationalist army was on the run. Peasants joined the Communist army by the tens of thousands; defeated Guomindang troops often jumped sides as well. With 2.5 million troops under his command, Mao began taking the cities. Faced with complete defeat, Chiang retreated to the island of Taiwan, located just 120 miles off the coast of the mainland.

On October 1, 1949, Mao stood atop the thirty-five-foot-tall Gate of Heavenly Peace, at the edge of Tiananmen Square in the heart of Beijing, and declared in a high-pitched voice, "Thus begins a new era in the history of China. We, the four hundred and seventy-five million people of China, have now stood up."[13] Standing with him were most of the heroes of the Communist victory, including Zhou Enlai, foreign minister; Zhu De, commander in chief of the military; Liu Shaoqi, vice chairman and soon-to-be president of the government; and Lin Biao, celebrated army commander.

As he looked out across a sea of hundreds of thousands of faces, Mao observed thousands of large red flags and banners flapping in the crisp autumn sky; and everywhere people waved signs with the slogans "Long Live Chairman Mao" and "Long Live the People's Republic of China." The band struck up the new national anthem, "The March of the Volunteers," and a seemingly endless parade of dancers and bands representing most of the nation's ethnic minorities, as well as soldiers of the People's Liberation Army, streamed past Mao and his new government. Mao had completed China's first step in its transition into the modern world. Only time would determine if he could succeed in the second step of strengthening his nation by building a strong economy.

The People's Republic of China and Mao's Legacy 2

Now that Mao Zedong and the CCP had established the People's Republic of China, the new leadership faced the massive task of constructing a modern nation out of the ruins left by years of war. There was a new enthusiasm in the air kindled by Mao's victory. For the first time since the 1911 revolution, the people had hope for a better future. The first task Mao and the CCP faced was to attend to a shattered economy.

Stabilizing the Economy

China's economy had been in disarray for more than a decade. Inflation was out of control, industrial output was 46 percent less than its peak before the war, and food output was around 30 percent of its prewar peak. The CCP's first move was to issue new currency, the renminbi. Next, they nationalized the banking system, thereby controlling credit. Salaries were stabilized and workers were paid in food and supplies instead of money. To manage production and distribution of goods, the government created and controlled trade organizations.

Mao faced a different problem in the countryside. After 1949 rich landlords, about 10 percent of the people, still owned almost 80 percent of the farmland. Rarely, however, did they work their own land, and this earned them the enmity of the Communists. O. Edmund Clubb, the U.S. consul general in Beijing in 1950, observed that most landlords "lived, in the market town or the county seat, on the rentals from the lands and had consequently been cast among the damned as 'non-people.'"[14]

In June 1950 Mao's Agrarian Reform Law set in motion the elimination of most private ownership of land. With CCP guidance, village peasants' associations denounced landlords, held public trials, and pronounced sentence. The penalty for being a landlord was harsh: An estimated 1.5 to 2 million landlords were put to death.

Everything related to production—land, farm animals, farm machinery, even surplus grain—was confiscated by the government and marked for redistribution. Peasants were categorized according to their wealth: rich (10 percent), middle (about 20 percent), and poor (70 percent). Generally, poor peasants received more land, animals, and equipment than the middle and rich peasants. By the end of 1952 almost all farming land had been redistributed to the peasants. Land reform appeared to boost productivity. The year that land reform was completed, agricultural production was more than 75 percent greater than it had been in 1949, the year the People's Republic was proclaimed.

A former landlord is tried and sentenced to death after Mao's Agrarian Reform Law eliminated most private ownership of land.

Industrial Policy

The CCP hoped to use the nation's agriculture to finance a massive industrial buildup. Farmers were forced to sell crops to the government at artificially low prices. The grain was then sold by the government for a profit and that money was used to build new factories or expand existing ones. Thanks to this shifting of resources, China's industry grew an average rate of 11.3 percent annually.

Not only did China's industry expand, but that expansion also resulted in the development of parts of the country that had been previously ignored. Mao worried that the United States, which had sided with Chiang Kaishek, would attack China's

A Chinese factory. During Mao's massive industrial undertaking called the Third Line, many industrial plants, roads, and bridges were built.

ports and vulnerable inland cities, so he mandated the removal of heavy industry from parts of eastern China to the far southwest and western provinces of Sichuan, Guizhou, Shaanxi, and Gansu. Tunnels were blasted through hundreds of miles of mountains to expand railroads thousands of miles through wilderness and deserts; roads and bridges were built where people had rarely ventured. The construction never ended, and new towns were created to serve plants relocated from back east. Millions of people were forced to move hundreds of miles to new homes as well. Unfortunately, this effort, known as the Third Line, was ruinously expensive. According to China expert Harrison E. Salisbury, "No project of Mao's reign was to prove so costly, so labor-intensive, so economically unfeasible, or so disruptive as the Third Line."[15]

Strengthening Party Control

Events on China's borders, meanwhile, provided an opportunity for Mao to strengthen his political position. Although the outbreak of war in Korea in 1950 between Communists and non-Communists, caught Mao by surprise, he took advantage of the hostilities to clamp down on his political enemies at home. Claiming that the war in Korea was evidence that communism was vulnerable to attack, in February 1951 he ordered the arrest and punishment of those who opposed Communist rule. Newspapers, all CCP controlled, published daily lists of those who had been executed and their supposed crimes. In the first six months of 1951 alone, 800,000 people were tried and 135,000 were executed. Hundreds of thousands of others were sentenced to hard labor or were placed under the supervision of party officials.

About the same time, Mao initiated what he called the Three-Antis Campaign, which attacked corruption and waste within the government. As many as a million party members were expelled. Another drive, called the Five-Antis Campaign, focused on further reducing the private ownership of businesses. Historian John King Fairbank explains that, "under the charges of bribery, tax evasion, theft of state assets, cheating in labor or materials, and stealing of state economic intelligence, nearly every employer could be brought to trial. The aim was to get control of the factories and squeeze capital out of the capitalists."[16]

These crackdowns enabled the party to solidify its control over China. Typically the CCP established political groups to advise government offices at the national, provincial, county, and village levels. In addition, at each production unit, whether it was a factory or a farm cooperative, the CCP appointed advisers who supervised the education and training of workers. Since CCP ideology held that politics and social life were inseparable, the party formed nationwide organizations governing activities from arts to sports. As a result, virtually no aspect of life was beyond the control of the Communist Party.

Collectivization

By 1955, despite potential enemies of Communist rule in China having been eliminated, the nation's economy was still far behind those of developed nations of the West. Agricultural production was barely keeping pace with population growth. To boost production, Mao decided to begin a program of collectivization in the countryside. Large farms—collectives—were created by pooling the land, tools, animals, and machines that previously had belonged to individual farmers.

These farms consisted of about 250 households, approximately 1,200 people. Administrators determined production, pricing, and distribution of crops; workers were paid wages. The new system offered China's government several advantages. The government was able to control production and collect taxes more easily. In addition, government could see to it that new technology was introduced faster, in theory enabling farms to increase production. Another benefit was that government services, such as health care and education, could be delivered more efficiently.

The change did not work out as planned, however. Peasants resented losing control of their equipment and work animals, and many killed their animals and sold them for meat instead. China specialist Jasper Becker writes that in the Anhui province, for example, records indicate that "the collective paid a peasant only

5.5 yuan for an ox but by selling it for meat he could earn 30 or 40 yuan."[17] Furthermore, peasants worked only hard enough to get their pay. A popular folk verse during the period illustrates the peasants' dissatisfaction with the communes: "Commune work, drag your feet, / When noontime comes, let's go and eat."[18]

Party leaders soon realized the need for reforms, so they reduced the size of collectives to approximately 170 households. Hoping to stimulate production, the CCP decreased taxes and also lowered the amount of grain the peasants were required to sell to the government at artificially low prices. In addition, the government allowed peasants to cultivate private plots and sell their harvest at private markets. But these concessions reduced government income, and as a result, the government had less money to fuel further industrial development.

A family works on a farm. Mao's program of collectivization combined the land, animals, and equipment of individual farms to form larger communal farms.

Mao Versus the Conservatives

Economic policies like collectivization of agriculture generated strong opposition to Mao. His opponents agreed that China should continue on the socialist path, but they generally favored a slower pace of change. They also objected to Mao's autocratic style of decision making. They favored rule by consensus rather than dictatorship. Mao's foremost critic was Liu Shaoqi, who was next in line of authority and who described Mao's collective policy as "false, dangerous, and utopian agrarian socialism."[19]

Many high party officials and a majority of bureaucrats shared Liu's opinion. At its Eighth National Party Congress in 1956, the CCP took action to dilute Mao's power. In the past, the party's Central Committee, which normally considered major policies for the future, had been entirely under Mao's chairmanship. The CCP created four Central Committee vice chairmanships and appointed four conservatives to the posts, among them Zhou Enlai and Liu Shaoqi. Then the party established the new position of secretary-general of the CCP to conduct the party's daily affairs and handed that position to Deng Xiaoping, an old comrade of Mao's.

Within the Politburo, a group consisting of approximately 10 percent of the Central Committee, an even more elite corps called the Standing Committee of the Politburo was created. Besides Mao, the party named the four conservative vice-chairmen of the Central Committee and the party's secretary-general, all opponents of the extreme measures being pushed by Mao, to the Standing Committee. The party put Liu Shaoqi and Deng Xiaoping in charge of the daily affairs of the country, and Mao reluctantly accepted this decision. To preserve the illusion that the party was unified, the conservatives muted their criticism of Mao.

The Great Leap Forward

The decade that followed was one of great instability as Mao used his remaining power to fight back against his opponents. In campaigns such as the Hundred Flowers Campaign, Mao smoked out as many as a million party members as well as thousands of intellectuals who openly criticized him. Mao also launched "the Great Leap Forward" to realize his dream of converting China's countryside into a model for Communist economic policy. The collectives were consolidated into approximately twenty-six thousand communes, each with approximately five thousand households, or nearly twenty-five thousand people. Communes were divided into brigades of about two hundred households, or a thousand persons. Brigades were broken down into production teams of a little over one hundred people each. The commune owned all property except for personal belongings. Families were allowed to live in their own houses, but single adults were housed in dormitories. All the people ate their meals in communal dining facilities.

By mid-1958 almost the entire agrarian population belonged to communes. However, they were doomed to fail. Poor management, ineffective farming methods, lack of motivation on the part of workers, and inflated production figures were among the many problems. To impress higher authorities, commune leaders lied about their grain production, reporting double or triple their actual harvest. When the government demanded grain as payment of taxes based on those reports, local authorities would comply, in the process taking almost everything from the peasants. With an insufficient supply of grain for communal kitchens, the people had to eat gruel made from wild grasses and scraps such as peanut shells and sweet potato skins. Almost all peasants ended up eating bark they peeled from trees.

Between 1958 and 1961 China suffered an estimated 30 to 40 million deaths from starvation and disease. Even Mao knew the country was in deep trouble, so when the rest of the CCP's leaders called on Deng Xiaoping and Liu Shaoqi to solve the problems created by the Great Leap Forward, Mao waited in the background, waiting for the opportunity to fight his way back to the top.

Mao's Comeback

By 1962 the economy had recovered under Liu's and Deng's leadership. However, the sixty-nine-year-old Mao was already

Great Leap Backward

In launching the Great Leap Forward, Mao demonstrated his belief that the masses could build China into a modern nation by sheer muscle and willpower. He ordered communes to send gangs of laborers into the countryside to work day and night on projects to construct and repair bridges, dams, irrigation systems, and roads. Work on the vast majority of these projects was of such inferior quality that many would deteriorate and collapse within a few years.

Another of Mao's brainchildren, the backyard furnace campaign, was a similar failure. In 1958 Mao required each commune to produce steel. He thought the steel could be used to make consumer products, freeing industry to concentrate on larger items, such as tractors and generators and construction materials. By the end of 1958, almost 100 million peasants were working ten to fifteen hours a day at backyard steel smelters. After a couple of years, Mao quietly ordered that the backyard furnaces be abandoned because the steel was so inferior it was useless.

plotting revenge against the "Revisionists," as he called Liu, Deng, and their supporters. He condemned them for turning China backward toward capitalism. In January 1965 Mao told the CCP Politburo that class struggle between capitalists and socialists was happening before their eyes within the party itself. Those who opposed him, Mao said, were taking the capitalists' road by resisting communism. Mao was enormously popular with the people of China, so direct, public opposition to him was futile. And most important, Mao had the utmost respect and support of the nation's military. Therefore, Liu, Deng, and their allies had to redirect Mao's plans, water them down, and delay them with amendments without letting the public see the bitter struggle that was going on behind the scenes.

For their part, the people blamed problems in the countryside on Mao's opponents, never on Mao, and he encouraged this attitude. By the mid-1960s pictures of Mao were displayed on the walls of homes and businesses. On one of his many visits to China, journalist Edgar Snow observed that in 1965, "giant portraits of him [Mao] now hung in the streets, busts were in every chamber, his books and photographs were everywhere on display to the exclusion of others. In the four-hour revolutionary pageant of dance and song, *The East Is Red*, Mao was the only hero. . . . The one-man cult was not yet universal, but the trend was unmistakable."[20]

The Great Proletarian Cultural Revolution

Many historians consider Mao's speech to the Politburo in January 1965, called the "Twenty-three Articles," to be the beginning of what came to be called the Cultural Revolution. Mao called for the formation of peasant organizations not controlled by party officials that would investigate and pass judgment on those accused of being "capitalist roaders." The lines of battle were drawn between the two sides: moderates, led by Liu Shaoqi and Deng Xiaoping, and the radicals, led by the Cultural Revolution Group (CRG), originally formed by Mao in late

A group of women look at a large portrait of Mao. In the mid-1960s, pictures of Mao were commonly posted in homes, businesses, and in public places.

1964 to "purify" the arts of capitalist influences. In 1965 the CRG was reorganized and expanded with Mao supporters.

The CRG backed a Beijing University philosophy instructor, Nie Yuanzi, who put up a poster calling for her colleagues to "unite and hold high the great red banner of Mao Tse-tung's thought. . . . Resolutely, thoroughly, totally and completely wipe out all monsters and demons and all counterrevolutionary revisionists."[21] Mao had the poster published in the *People's Daily*, the government-sponsored newspaper, and broadcast on radio.

Liu and Deng still thought they could work around Mao's directives, but Nie Yuanzi's poster had stirred students' discontent. As the student demonstrations and turmoil spread in June, Liu and Deng flew to Hangzhou, where Mao was living, to ask for advice. They asked him to return to Beijing and take control of the disorder. Mao answered that he had no intention of traveling to Beijing and told them to "solve the problem according to the situation in the movement."[22]

A month later, however, Mao was ready to make his move and returned to Beijing. On July 18 he addressed the party there, scolding members for their fear of conflict. There must be revolution, he admonished.

Red Guards

Mao formally launched the Cultural Revolution on August 1, 1966, at a meeting of the party's Central Committee, calling for a war on what he called the Four Olds: old ideas, old culture, old customs, and old habits of the exploiting classes. He dismissed Liu Shaoqi as party vice chairman and demoted him from second to eighth on the Politburo chain of command. Lin Biao was named the only vice chairman of the Politburo, making him the second most powerful man in the country. During this meeting, Mao recognized a group called the Red Guards, saying that these "brave vanguards . . . of revolutionary youngsters . . . are airing their views and opinions in a big way, exposing and criticizing in a big way, firmly launching an attack against the open and covert representatives of the bourgeoisie."[23]

More than one million Red Guards pack Tiananmen Square on August 18, 1966, waving their red bound copies of Quotations from Chairman Mao *in the air as he passes.*

The young people responded to his speech with exuberance. More than a million Red Guards from around China packed Tiananmen Square on August 18, 1966, wearing khaki uniforms and red armbands inscribed with the words *Red Guard*. Waving their red, plastic-bound *Quotations from Chairman Mao* high in the air, they cheered the seventy-three-year-old Mao as he stood on the upper gallery of Tiananmen Gate, the Gate of Heavenly Peace.

The Red Guards spread across China, attacking anything they associated with either traditional Chinese culture or Western culture. They burned books published in China before 1949 and any book written by Western authors. They raided the homes of those they suspected of opposing Mao and his Cultural Revolution. The homes' occupants were paraded through the streets wearing dunce caps and signs around their necks listing their supposed crimes. The more unfortunate targets were beaten and left to suffer or die without help. In just a couple of months, hundreds of thousands of men and women had been harassed in some way by the Red Guards. Because they had Mao's blessing, the Red Guards met very little resistance from the party and police.

The Origin of the Red Guards

Teenagers throughout China joined together to form militant groups that came to be known as Red Guards. The idea, Harrison E. Salisbury writes in his book *The New Emperors*, came to Mao Zedong in the spring of 1966. Speaking to Kang Sheng, the head of the secret police and a member of the Cultural Revolution Committee, Mao alluded to the allegorical tale of the Monkey King, a rebellious monkey and folk hero in Chinese literature who upset the gods in heaven. Mao said, "We must overthrow the king of hell and liberate the little devils. We need more Monkeys to disrupt the royal palace." From this conversation, Kang initiated the Red Guards.

Through undercover agents throughout the universities and high schools, Kang sent word to organize the youth. Soon large groups of students wearing red armbands with white letters spelling out *Red Guard* were gathering to defend Mao Zedong's teachings, even if it meant their deaths. They carried with them a short one-volume edition of the *Quotations from Chairman Mao* published in 1966 by Lin Biao.

Rebellious teenagers like these were recruited into the Red Guards by undercover agents.

The unity of the revolutionaries soon broke down, and by early 1967 the Red Guards had split into two major factions. One was more moderate, looking to reform the party as much as to punish those who had strayed from Mao's teachings. The other was much more radical, taking literally Mao's call for the masses to attack wayward party members. These radicals intended to reorganize society from the bottom up.

China now stood on the verge of anarchy. Loyal only to Mao Zedong and his teachings, the radicals began taking over factories, slowing down production as a result. Thousands of Red Guard organizations existed with no central authority. Some were arming themselves and were battling against each other. Mao said to Zhou Enlai, "China is now like a country divided into 800 princely states."[24]

Mao Calls for Order

Concerned that his Cultural Revolution was out of control, by the spring of 1967 Mao was calling for the Red Guards to take immediate steps to restore order in the nation. Most party officials, he proclaimed, were loyal revolutionaries. Perhaps some of them had drifted away from the party's doctrine from time to time, but most of those could be reformed. Mao then called on Lin Biao and the army for help in restoring order.

Essentially, the military was supposed to be taking charge. However, the army itself began to divide into factions. A conservative law-and-order group in Beijing supported Mao; and more radical, regional forces wanted to continue organizing workers and students to eliminate "counterrevolutionaries" from society. In July 1967, in the central industrial city of Wuhan, civil war nearly broke out during a tense standoff between traditional party leaders and a breakaway People's Liberation Army (PLA) division supporting radical workers. Zhou Enlai flew down to mediate, but the radical forces refused to let his plane land. The radicals backed down only after Lin Biao dispatched three infantry divisions and navy gunboats and threatened to attack.

By mid-1967 resistance to Mao within the party had crumbled under the pressure of mass criticism. Mao's top two enemies, Liu Shaoqi and Deng Xiaoping, were under heavy guard. Mao now believed it was time to restore order, but the fighting continued. During the spring of 1968 bloody battles between the PLA and radical Red Guards broke out. Fighting and more deaths occurred on university campuses during that summer. In late July Mao called together some representatives of the Politburo, including four who had backed the Cultural Revolution and five Beijing Red Guard leaders, and scolded them for their excesses. Mao told them, "We want cultural struggle, not armed struggle."[25]

Mao eventually quelled the turmoil of the Cultural Revolution by sending as many as 50 million young people to the countryside so they could work with and learn from the peasants. He then increased PLA influence in the party by appointing more military personnel to high positions. By 1969 PLA soldiers made up 49 percent of the Central Committee; two-

Liu Shaoqi: Enemy Number One

Although Mao had designated Liu Shaoqi as his successor in the 1950s, by the mid-1960s Mao had labeled Liu the nation's number-one "bad" element. As the Cultural Revolution picked up steam in September 1966, Liu lived under virtual house arrest in his Zongnanhai government compound home. The Red Guard's verbal attacks and public humiliation of his family went on almost nonstop. On August 8, 1967, Liu and his wife were dragged onto a stage in front of thousands and were tortured. In front of film crews, Red Guards beat and kicked Liu and his wife for two hours, dragged them home, then separated and beat them again. Both were badly injured. The beatings continued, and Liu, most of his teeth gone and deprived of his diabetes medicine, grew sicker. He could barely eat, slept only an hour or two at night, and suffered from infections.

Under the supervision of Jiang Qing, hundreds of people were tortured and even killed by investigators who were trying to find evidence to use against Liu. By October Liu had to be tube fed. Liu lived connected to tubes, barely able to utter a word, and in immense pain for another year. On October 1, 1969, he was removed to the city of Kaifeng in the Henan province.

Historian Harrison Salisbury describes the scene of Liu's death in his book *The New Emperors*: "Liu Shaoqi, on feeding tubes and drip medication, was wrapped naked in a cotton blanket, loaded onto a plane, and flown to remote Kaifeng. . . . He died there on November 12, 1969, lying naked on the cement floor in the basement of an old prison. . . . Unshaven, his hair uncut for months, Liu had died of pneumonia."

thirds of the fifteen hundred delegates to the Ninth National Party Congress held that April wore military uniforms.

Mao's Last Years

Besides the chaos within China, Mao was also worried about the potential for conflict with China's neighbor to the northwest, the Soviet Union. During 1969 troops from China and the Soviets had fought brief skirmishes because of a border dispute in northern Manchuria. Mao and Zhou Enlai worked to defuse the Sino-Soviet crisis by agreeing to a cease-fire and negotiations over their border dispute.

Mao and Zhou decided they could also curb the Soviets by opening up relations with the United States. The problem was that the United States had never recognized the Communists as the legitimate government of China, choosing instead to deal with Chiang Kaishek and his government in Taiwan. Zhou and the head of America's National Security Council, Henry Kissinger, worked out an agreement in November 1971 that sidestepped who was the legitimate ruler of China, saying, "The United States acknowledges that all Chinese on either side of the Taiwan Strait maintain there is but one China. The United States government does not challenge that position."[26] This agreement paved the way for a historic visit to China by U.S. president Richard Nixon. On February 21, 1972, Mao met privately with Nixon, helping to mend a split that dated back to World War II.

Mao's health had deteriorated rapidly by then. Seeing that the end of his long reign was near, several contenders for Mao's position maneuvered behind the scenes, leaving Mao with few allies he could trust. Some individuals, in fact, had proven unwilling to wait for Mao's death. For example, Lin Biao had recently died in a plane crash as he was fleeing China following Mao's discovery of Lin's plot for a coup d'état. To conduct the day-to-day affairs of government, Mao turned to the one comrade he knew he could trust, Zhou Enlai. At Zhou's urging, Mao restored Deng Xiaoping to government service, and in February 1973 Deng returned to join Zhou in the heavy task of stabilizing and building up China's economy.

President Richard Nixon (left) and Mao meet privately on February 21, 1972, to mend relations between the United States and China.

Zhou's and Deng's moderation was seen as a threat by the radicals who had formed the core of the Cultural Revolution Group. Led by Mao's wife, Jiang Qing, Zhang Chunqiao, Yao Wenyuan, and Wang Hongwen defended the extremist ideas of the Cultural Revolution. All four were members of the Communist Party's Politburo, and Zhang and Wang were members of the Standing Committee. Zhou was seriously ill with cancer and was no real threat to Jiang. Jiang realized that Deng was a legitimate rival. Mao, however, had soured of Jiang and her clique, so for a time he backed Deng. He described Jiang, Wang, Zhang, and Yao as a "Gang of Four," who had too much ambition and who should listen more to the party. Mao told his wife in November, "Don't show your face too much. Don't write instructions or comments on documents. You are not to form the cabinet from backstage. You have stirred up widespread resentment. You should unite with the majority."[27]

The Lin Biao Affair

In the late 1960s Lin Biao, head of the People's Liberation Army, was next in line to replace the aging Mao Zedong as the head of the country. When Lin became suspicious that Mao was resurrecting the power of the party while downplaying the role of the military, Lin decided to make a move. At a meeting of the Central Committee in August 1970, Lin attacked Premier Zhou Enlai's domestic and foreign policies even though Mao had issued a communiqué that defended Zhou's new foreign policy of peaceful coexistence with other nations.

To further his cause, Lin tried to maneuver himself to be appointed president of the country, a top position left vacant after Liu Shaoqi had died in prison. Lin tried to flatter Mao by proposing that the Politburo declare that Mao Zedong thought was more important than Communist Party doctrine. By this time, however, Mao had lost faith in Lin and dismissed his proposal. Instead, Mao reinforced the idea of the party's role as the leader of revolution.

Lin and some army allies were plotting to assassinate Mao by bombing his train. When he got word that Mao knew of the plot, Lin tried to escape. The plane carrying Lin and his family crashed mysteriously in September 1971 in Mongolia, killing all aboard. Lin's death was followed by a purge of many of the top military and civilian officials. Eleven of the twenty-one members of the party Politburo were dismissed, as Mao eliminated anyone who might have been sympathetic with Lin.

Although Mao and Lin Biao appeared together in public, there was great tension between the two men.

As his own health deteriorated, however, Mao vacillated between support for Zhou's and Deng's views and those of the Gang of Four. Eventually, recalling Deng's long opposition to his economic policies, Mao unleashed the Gang of Four to resume their attacks on Zhou and Deng.

Meanwhile, after a series of operations for his cancer, Zhou died on January 8, 1976. The nation mourned throughout the spring. Despite Mao's orders that the public not be allowed to mourn, a million people assembled at Tiananmen Square to watch Zhou's cortege pass on its way to the crematorium. Then, on April 5, the traditional festival of Qing Ming (the day for commemorating dead ancestors), huge demonstrations of support for Zhou's policies occurred throughout the country.

The Gang of Four refused to give up their efforts to take charge of the government. They publicly attacked Deng Xiaoping, accusing him of promoting the mourning for Zhou and intending to reverse all of Mao's programs. Relieved of his positions again, Deng slipped out of Beijing and waited quietly for a chance to overthrow the Gang of Four.

The Fall of the Gang of Four and the Resurrection of Deng Xiaoping

Mao died on September 9, 1976. Soon after, the Gang of Four demanded that the Politburo expel Deng from the party and name Jiang Qing as party chairwoman. That effort was unsuccessful. Instead, the Politburo named another protégé of Mao's, Hua Guofeng, as party chairman and premier of the nation. The Gang of Four plotted to overthrow the government, but Hua uncovered their plans and ordered their arrest.

With the defeat of the Gang of Four, the way was cleared for Deng to return to public life. By July 1977 Deng, with strong public support and backing from the military, had regained all of the positions in the party that he had lost—deputy chairman of the Central Committee, vice chairman of the Military Committee, and positions on the Politburo and the Standing Committee. Deng also was appointed vice premier of the National People's Congress and chief of staff of the PLA.

Over the next several months, Deng and Hua Guofeng argued about China's future during Politburo meetings. Because of his pragmatic approach to solving economic problems, the majority in the Politburo decided to support Deng as China's next leader. Deng worked behind the scenes, promoting his supporters into the majority on China's two main power organizations: the Central Committee and the Politburo. His ascent to power marked a dramatic shift from the one-man rule of Mao to a collective leadership that would work out problems in secret and then present decisions with a unified voice. With the chaos of the Cultural Revolution and the uncertainty over who would run China behind them, Deng and his comrades could get down to the business of solving their nation's many problems.

Deng Xiaoping's Black-and-White Economic Cats 3

Deng Xiaoping's position as China's leader was enhanced by the near-universal respect he commanded. His integrity and his vision for modernizing China earned the respect of the entire nation. The army respected him because of his military service during World War II. Party members respected him because of his intense loyalty to and long service in the Communist Party. The people loved him because they associated him with Zhou Enlai and because Deng had always promoted programs that benefited the people.

After twenty-six years of Mao Zedong's rule, the vast majority of Chinese still suffered from poverty. Deng, with his practical approach to leadership, was ideally suited to solving his nation's problems. Deng's down-to-earth approach toward reviving China's failing economy had been foretold in his 1961 address to the party's Central Committee: "It does not matter whether the cat is black or white. So long as it catches the mouse it is a good cat."[28] In other words, capitalism and socialism both would be held to the same standard: How well they served the Chinese people.

Political Rehabilitation and Party Reform

Beyond reviving China's economy, Deng's other ambition was to build the Communist Party into a professional, vital political force with college-educated leaders who understood the complexities of the modern age. Thousands of men and women who had been victims of Mao's or the Gang of Four's persecution were appointed to top administrative positions, including Hu Yaobang to lead the CCP and Zhao Ziyang to be premier of the State Council. Both men had suffered persecution during the Cultural Revolution. As historian Ross Terrill writes, "In some ways Deng's China grew directly from the ashes of Mao's. Half the Politburo for much of the 1980s consisted of people whom Mao had imprisoned or sent to rural labor. Half the small businessmen who make the economy zip are former inmates of Mao's prisons and labor camps."[29]

Deng took over in 1978 with the overwhelming support from the public. People believed Deng's promises to create a socialist democracy and to reform the legal system. Soon wall posters appeared around Beijing expressing new hopes for democracy and freedom. The activists called democracy "the fifth modernization," connecting it to an earlier program of Zhou Enlai's, the Four Modernizations: the development of agriculture, industry, national defense, and science and technology, a program that Deng strongly advocated as well.

Deng Xiaoping took power in 1978 with the overwhelming support of the Chinese people.

Before long, however, Deng and party officials began to see the public debate over government policies as a threat to their leadership. Deng felt that any social instability would hamper China's economic revival. He said, "Our people have just gone through a decade of suffering. . . . [They] cannot afford further chaos."[30] With Deng's blessing, the government banned publications and organizations not authorized by the party. Arrests of the more prominent spokespersons followed, and the demonstrations ended. Deng was confident that the vast majority of Chinese people would forget politics if they could become richer. And he was at least partly right. The people welcomed the opportunity to improve their lives.

Agricultural Reform

Deng began his economic reform in the countryside with the Household Responsibility System (HRS) program. Deng's plan was to begin eliminating communes and instead give each household a private plot of land to farm. At harvest time, once they paid their taxes with their crops, households could sell any surplus in free markets. This plan would finally liberate the peasants because now they could grow as much as they wanted, pay their taxes, and keep the money they earned by selling their surplus at competitive prices.

As a result of Deng's agricultural reforms, agricultural production and household income rose steadily. Between 1978 and 1984, agricultural output grew by an average of 9 percent per year. In addition, peasants finally had enough money to purchase items to make their lives more comfortable. Between 1978 and 1982, peasants' annual income rose from an average of about $65 to $135. With this increased income, peasant families were able to build new brick houses instead of mud and straw ones. They were able to upgrade their farm equipment and buy more consumer goods, such as televisions and videocassette recorders, which government-owned stores sold at affordable prices.

Rural Industry

Another of Deng's innovations was to permit individuals to open up side businesses to supplement their farm income. This was a key change since half of the 400 million potential workers in the countryside could not make a decent living off of the land because the plots were only large enough for subsistence farming. All over China, peasants set up businesses that processed food, made and sold chemical fertilizers, offered transportation, and made cement

The Official Word on Mao's Career

In June 1981 Deng presented an extensive evaluation of Mao Zedong's career, which appears in volume 2 of *Selected Works of Deng Xiaoping*. He talked of Mao as an equal among party officials, referring to him as "comrade." Mao's great leadership and thought had led the people to liberation and national pride, Deng contended. Deng rejected pressure from many officials who wanted to condemn Mao thoroughly. Mao had made mistakes, Deng admitted, but so had everyone in the Communist Party:

> When we talk about mistakes, we should not speak only of Comrade Mao, for many other leading comrades in the Central Committee made mistakes too. Comrade Mao got carried away when we launched the Great Leap Forward, but didn't the rest of us go along with him? Neither Comrade Liu Shaoqi nor Comrade Zhou Enlai nor I for that matter objected to it, and [Central Committee member] Comrade Chen Yun didn't say anything either. We must be fair on these questions and not give the impression that only one individual made mistakes while everybody else was correct, because it doesn't tally with the facts.

for construction. Soon sideline activities became the major source of income for millions of families and village wealth increased accordingly. In the Sichuan province, for example, the income earned in the village of Fenghuang was $50,000 in 1977. By 1984 the village's total income was $1.5 million.

These economic reforms had a downside, however. Because farmers made more money growing fruits and vegetables, they grew less grain and cotton. With the decline in grain production in 1985, China had to import more grain to feed its people. Furthermore, by the mid-1980s, the growth in farm income began to slow. The government solution was to encourage even more small businesses, called township and village enterprises (TVEs). These TVEs were normally very small, with fewer than ten workers.

TVEs proved popular, and as their number surged, farming became less popular. But there were too few jobs for the tens of millions of peasants leaving the farms. Believing they could find jobs away from the farms, millions of peasants became a floating population of migrant laborers. These migrants were often poorly educated and unskilled. As a result, the majority of migrants ended up working at low-paying, often temporary jobs in cities.

The Urban Economy

Even as migrants headed for the cities, the government faced the problem of an inefficient urban economy where a third of the state-owned enterprises (SOEs) were losing money. Deng decided that factories and businesses would be more productive if the government left more decision making up to individual managers. Deng turned planning and decision making over to the local managers. Now managers would establish their own production, marketing, and staffing plans. Successful managers could apply their company profits to providing benefit packages or bonuses for workers, invest in plant expansion, or even open up other businesses.

These were radical changes not just for managers but for workers, who were accustomed to guaranteed jobs until they retired, free health care, and pensions. Workers' benefits also included subsidized housing, free child care, free schooling for children, and guaranteed jobs for children when their parents retired. Deng proposed that these benefits be phased out. New workers would be given contracts for limited periods, and their wages would be based on performance. Those who performed best would be offered renewed contracts, but no longer could people take having a job for granted. Benefits for these newer workers were limited to on-the-job medical coverage.

Deng also recognized that part of what had prevented SOEs from making money was that prices they could charge for products were set at artificially low levels by the government. Deng decided to open prices on thousands of products to free-market

The Trial of the Gang of Four

To create a Communist Party that the people would trust, Deng first had to close the book on the Gang of Four, the radical Communists responsible for much of the suffering during the Cultural Revolution. People across China watched recorded segments of the two-month trial on television. Prosecutors condemned gang members—who were locked inside iron cages during the trial—for dozens of crimes, from plots to overthrow the government to persecution of seven hundred thousand people that resulted in thirty-four thousand deaths.

Historian Maurice Meisner writes in his book *Mao's China and After* that "the most important political purpose for the highly ritualized spectacle was to raise the question of the role of Mao Zedong in the events for which his widow and one time comrades stood condemned as criminals." Jiang Qing, Mao's widow and the most hated of the four, snapped defiantly, "I was Chairman Mao's dog. Whomever he told me to bite, I bit." The chief prosecutor appeared to agree on this point when he closed his case, stating that the people "are very clear that Chairman Mao was responsible . . . for their plight during the Cultural Revolution." After the conviction of the Gang of Four, at least the Chinese people felt partial satisfaction that some justice had been achieved.

Mao's widow, Jiang Qing, was sentenced to death at the trial of the Gang of Four.

competition. Prices would fluctuate according to supply and demand. To prevent immediate price increases that would lead to social unrest, Deng decided to keep prices on some products fixed, especially for staples such as rice and flour and crucial industrial products such as steel and oil. Other products were allowed to fluctuate, but only within government-set limits. Still, as expected, when the reforms were implemented in Beijing in 1985, the prices of eighteen hundred food items rose almost 50 percent. Some prices rose even more dramatically. For example, fish rose 200 percent, and pork went up 35 percent.

One effect of economic reform was the creation of new enterprises as people sought ways to bring in enough money to meet their needs. Workers often organized side businesses such as repair shops and restaurants. Vendors started selling food, clothing, watches, and other consumer goods along city streets. During the mid-1980s, these new enterprises expanded by as much as 20 percent annually and provided millions of jobs.

Opening the Door to the West

Deng also believed that China needed help in the form of Western technology and expertise to modernize. With this in mind, he announced a program called "Opening to the West." The centerpiece of the program was the creation of special economic zones (SEZs) along China's coast. In the SEZs, foreign companies and investors were invited to open high-tech factories and businesses and were offered cheap rent and tax advantages as added inducements.

The SEZs got off to a slow start. This was partly because foreign companies were skeptical about operating under China's complex laws and tangled bureaucracy. The businesses from overseas that did start up in the SEZs, however, found a well-educated labor force that would work for low wages. Willing to work long hours with little or no time off, the Chinese workers adapted to the new technology quickly.

There were advantages for the Chinese as well. Those with foreign-language skills worked as interpreters and advisers for

With little or no skills or education, many migrants found themselves working as vendors after leaving their villages and moving to the cities.

the foreign firms. These workers usually received excellent salaries, access to foreign stores, and better living conditions. Many younger Chinese with connections to the government were able to get money and assistance to open up businesses related to the new foreign companies, especially in the import/export field.

The Seeds of Disorder

Not everyone in leadership positions was happy with these reforms, however. Opening the economy to capitalism provided a tempting opportunity for party bureaucrats to get rich through direct investment or through political influence peddling. Often, family members of high party officials became wealthy. In 1985 some members of the Politburo attacked the SEZs. The various subsidies the government provided cost more money than the foreign companies brought in. Furthermore, the foreigners were bringing in too much Western popular culture, which some saw as ruining the values of young Chinese. Deng himself suggested that the SEZs had yet to prove their value. When asked in June 1985 by a visiting diplomat about the Shenzhen SEZ, Deng admitted that it "was an experiment. At this time we can still not say whether we have taken the correct path."[31]

Deng had to strike a balanced position between party conservatives who insisted that state planning and state-owned industry remain the cornerstone of China's economy and liberals who wanted to continue his market-oriented reforms. Both sides worried about inflation, which hit 25 percent in the cities by mid-1985. Yet no one wanted to return to the dreary lifestyles of the Mao era, so Deng was able to negotiate compromises between liberals and conservatives. Deng slowed the pace of his reforms, but he also closed many state factories that were losing money.

The combination of rising prices, reduced benefits, and unemployed workers led, not unexpectedly, to unrest. As had been true in the past, the protests began on the nation's college campuses. Student complaints included party and government corruption, unequal job opportunities, and inflation. By January 1987 students had demonstrated on more than 150 campuses in seventeen cities. Even more disturbing to the party, worker groups were joining the students. Deng moved quickly to quash the protests. A leading academician, Fang Lizhi, was expelled from the party and dismissed from his university post for inciting student protests. Liu Binyan, a *People's Daily* journalist well known for his exposés of party corruption, was dismissed from the newspaper and also expelled from the party.

To make sure political liberals understood his message, Deng dismissed party secretary Hu Yaobang for not suppressing the student demonstrations. Zhao Ziyang, a moderate, became secretary-general of the party; and a conservative party official, sixty-year-old Li Peng, was appointed premier of the State Council. Deng resigned all of his positions except the all-powerful chairmanship of the party's Central Military Com-

University students burn newspapers to protest party and government corruption, inflation, and unequal job opportunities.

mission. With sixty-eight-year-old Zhao in position as Deng's chosen successor, moderate forces were still in control, although conservatives still had a powerful voice in Li Peng.

Zhao continued with Deng's economic reforms, and industrial growth accelerated. For example, China's industry grew an impressive 21 percent in 1988 alone. Rapid growth, however, was accompanied by inflation. Conservative Politburo members voted to postpone further easing of controls on prices. In addition, they reestablished government control over many enterprises.

Economic and social problems multiplied. In the countryside, peasants suffered from a shortage of fertilizer and lower government prices for grain. As the rural economy soured, TVEs, which employed 100 million workers, had to cut back production and lay off employees. As many as 50 million unemployed peasants flooded cities looking for work. The cities themselves were already simmering with discontent. Work slowdowns and strikes became common. Furthermore, people were alarmed by the growth of youth gangs, gambling, prostitution, and drug addiction.

Deng Xiaoping now came to believe that his economic reforms had opened the gate to social changes that were endangering the nation's stability. Liberal dissenters, not hard-line Communists, Deng believed, now threatened his goal of bringing wealth to all of China.

Spring 1989: Tiananmen Demonstrations

Certainly, Deng had reason for concern as demonstrations against the government broke out on college campuses across China during the spring of 1989. One major complaint was the widespread corruption at all levels of government. In addition, university students were disgruntled because they were being forced to work in factories or on farms as part of their educational programs.

Deng Xiaoping was concerned that China might be headed for a disaster like that experienced during the Cultural Revolution. As early as February 1989, when U.S. president George Bush visited China, Deng had voiced his apprehensions: "If all one billion of us undertake multiparty elections, we will certainly run into a full-scale civil war."[32]

Dissent even found its way into the center of China's power structure. At a Politburo meeting in April, Hu Yaobang started reading a long list of complaints about government corruption and abuse of power. When Politburo members interrupted him, Hu angrily declared, "We have failed the people and nation."[33] But Hu was not destined to protect China's reforms. Shortly after delivering his speech, the seventy-three-year-old veteran party leader suffered a heart attack and died.

News of Hu's death provided a focal point for students' dissatisfaction. During the night, students laid wreaths in Hu's memory at the foot of the Monument to the Heroes of the Revolution in the middle of Tiananmen Square. For days, thousands of students demanding democratic reform were joined by workers in the square. Party officials feared mass demonstrations against the government. As a result, the public was forbidden to enter Tiananmen Square on April 22, the day Hu's funeral was to be held.

Despite the order, a hundred thousand students slipped into the square before the army could seal it off. At Hu's funeral, student leaders called for students across Beijing to boycott classes. The students dispersed following the funeral, but on April 26 the *People's Daily* published an editorial in which Deng, referring to the demonstrations, warned that if the government maintained "a lenient attitude toward this turmoil and just let it go, a situation of real chaos will emerge . . . and hope for reform and opening up . . . will be reduced to nothing."[34] Deng's warning infuriated student leaders, who had always taken care to show their patriotism.

Thousands of students and workers gather in Tiananmen Square in April 1989, demanding democratic reform.

Zhao Ziyang: Party Maverick

On April 27, in response to Deng's remarks, 150,000 students converged on Tiananmen Square demanding democratic reforms. For a time, the government tolerated the protesters, and some officials even expressed cautious support for them. Zhao Ziyang, for example, on May 4 told an Asian Development Bank meeting in Beijing that the "reasonable demands from the students should be met through democratic and legal means."[35]

The Tiananmen Incident

In June 1989 the CCP decided to end the three-month-long series of demonstrations in Tiananmen Square. Deng Xiaoping and his supporters called on troops to restore order. On June 3 a busload of military officers arrived at the square and demanded that the remaining students, only a few thousand, leave. When the students resisted, about a thousand PLA soldiers entered the square from the Great Hall of the People. Unknown to the demonstrators, these troops were just a diversion. In fact, an armed force of forty thousand troops, with tanks and troop carriers, had begun to move through major Beijing streets toward the square. When the army encountered citizens manning barricades of overturned cars and buses, the tanks fired, killing or wounding anyone in the way.

Armed battles broke out as the PLA advanced through the streets. Citizens who were incensed that the PLA would fire on the people flung Molotov cocktails at tanks and trucks, killing dozens of soldiers. Soldiers were dragged from their vehicles and beaten; many were killed. By the time the PLA reached Tiananmen Square at 2:30 A.M. on June 4, hundreds and possibly thousands of citizens and soldiers were already dead, and many thousands were injured.

To the dismay of the government, the battle was being broadcast by hundreds of radio and television reporters from around the world. Most of the media attention was still centered in the square, so the soldiers had orders to keep the violence down. First they destroyed as many cameras as possible to discourage filming and reporting of the crackdown. Then the PLA tore down the Goddess of Democracy statue and the tent city that had sheltered the demonstrators. Finally, around 6:20 A.M. on June 4, the PLA lined up the remaining five thousand students and marched them away.

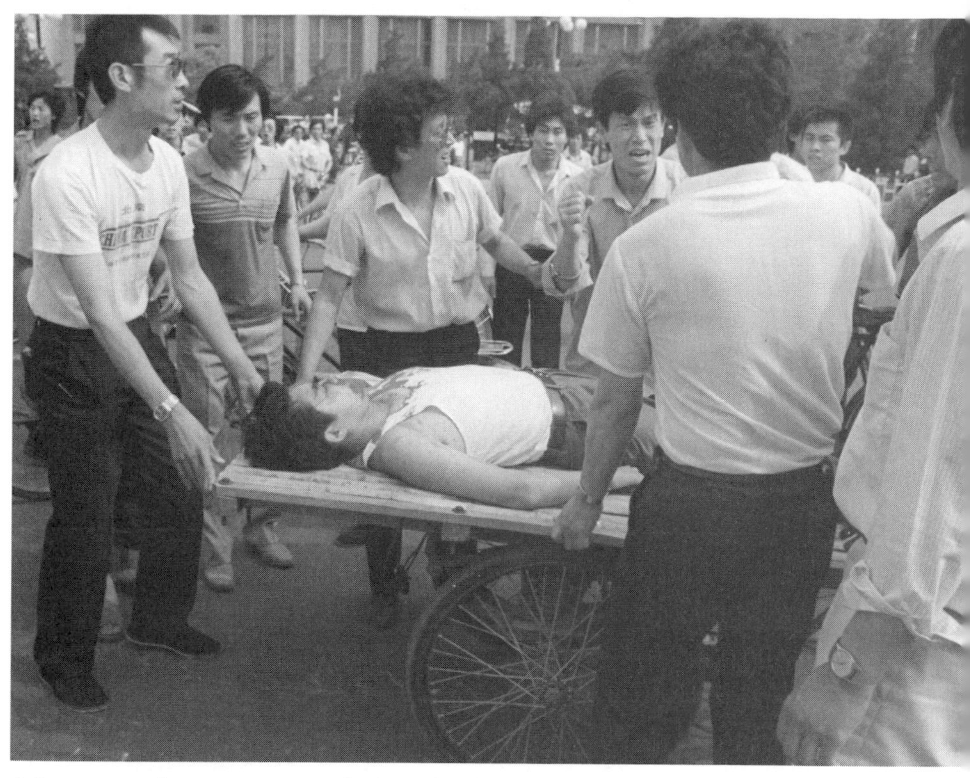

Many people were wounded and killed on June 3, 1989, when PLA troops backed by tanks opened fire on protesters in Tiananmen Square.

Government tolerance soon came to an end. When, on the occasion of a visit to China by Soviet leader Mikhail Gorbachev, half a million demonstrators gathered to protest against the Chinese government, Deng was humiliated. On May 18 the government declared that martial law was in effect, and less than three weeks later, on June 3, PLA troops moved in to clear Tiananmen Square.

The soldiers were heavily armed and accompanied by tanks. When citizens tried to block their progress, the soldiers began firing at the people, triggering a bloody night of fierce fighting between citizens and the army. On the morning of June 4 the streets were filled with wrecked and burning vehicles. Estimates of deaths from the fighting ranged between several hundred to several thousand.

The Political Aftermath

The incident in Tiananmen Square resulted in a major shakeup in the party and in society in general. Zhao was stripped of his party positions. But Deng allowed his longtime colleague to retreat into retirement under house arrest. Deng named Shanghai mayor Jiang Zemin the new party secretary. Thousands of Chinese, from government officials to college professors, were fired for their support of the student movement. Zhao Ziyang's chief aide, Bao Tong, was sentenced to seven years in prison. For a short period the government cracked down on publications. At the *People's Daily*, the editor in chief, director, three deputy chief directors, and forty-six reporters were fired. Dozens of book publishers were closed, and lists of banned authors circulated.

The Tiananmen Square incident left party members cynical about their leaders. Sinologist Orville Schell writes that a friend told him in 1990 that the people "know that they [government officials] are lying to us, and they know that we are lying to them. In fact, everybody knows that everyone is lying to everyone else. So you might say that the system is working just as it's supposed to."[36]

Back to Business

China's Communist Party publicly blamed Western nations for the violence at Tiananmen Square, saying they were corrupting Chinese society with capitalist ideas as a means of undermining socialism. Still, Deng made it clear that he would expand opportunities for people to get rich as long as they avoided embarrassing the party by demanding political change. And in the end, much of what China's leaders did to suppress dissent ceased to matter. As longtime China specialist Francesco Sisci writes,

> A great change in this attitude occurred after the June 4, 1989 Tiananmen Square event. In spite of the massive check on individual involvement in the pro-democracy movement, there was no major crackdown and punishment. The state also started withdrawing from its attentive

involvement in personal lives, and people gained more personal freedom that translated into more social freedom, more economic freedom and more freedom of expression. After 1992 and the 14th Party Congress, this trend became even more marked, with the new leadership working to reevaluate and promote people who were formerly involved in the June 4 movement.[37]

Developments in Rural China

Once the upheaval following the Tiananmen Square incident had subsided, China and its leaders concentrated on economic concerns. Even though China's overall economic growth continued to outpace that of most other nations, the benefits were not shared by all. In the countryside, peasants' income had begun decreasing in value in the late 1980s as a result of inflation. Pressed to earn more money to pay taxes and repay debts, families would often have to split up. One member would find work at a rural enterprise while another would go into a city in search of work.

To keep workers in rural areas, the government encouraged farmers to invest their money in developing local industries. This initiative resulted in the growth of small towns as people gravitated toward where jobs could be found. In 1992 China had twelve thousand rural towns, compared to about four thousand in 1978. New factories located in rural areas, such as the southern part of the Zhejiang province on China's coast, produced everything from electronics to machinery.

Regaining Lost Lands

Deng's objective of reviving China's economy was furthered by his success in regaining Chinese sovereignty over lands long held by foreign powers. Deng had stated early in his reign that he wanted to regain control of Hong Kong and Macao, which were held by Britain and Portugal, respectively. With its many banks, Hong Kong promised to be a rich source of capital for development projects elsewhere in China. Deng recognized it was in China's interest to keep the banks from pulling out of Hong Kong. The treaty by which Great Britain held most of Hong Kong was set to expire at midnight on June 30, 1997, and Deng was determined that the transition back to Chinese control be accomplished without causing a panic in this capitalist enclave.

In 1985 Great Britain agreed to Deng's One Country, Two Systems proposal, which included guarantees that the limited political freedoms of Hong Kong's residents would be respected. Under Chinese rule, Hong Kong would be allowed to retain its current economic and governing system for at least fifty years.

Two years later, in 1987, China and Portugal agreed to terms that would return Macao to Chinese control in 1999. Macao's return had less of an economic impact on China since its largest industry was tourism and the colony had never been a regional banking center as Hong Kong had been. Still, just as Hong Kong's return had been, regaining sovereignty over Macao was a major victory for Deng.

Taiwan

Deng attempted to work out a similar agreement with Taiwan, which had been at odds with China's government ever since Chiang Kaishek and his anti-Communist forces had fled there in 1949. Deng's spokesman, Ye Jiangyin, proposed a nine-point plan in 1981 that would have allowed Taiwan to retain its own social, economic, and military systems. The plan included the idea of One Country, Two Systems as a resolution to the stalemate between the two countries, but Taiwan continued to reject any agreement that would have placed the island under the control of the People's Republic of China. The issue of Taiwan's status would continue to unsettle not just relations between the island and the mainland but also between China and the other world powers, including the United States.

Despite the failure of Deng to regain control of Taiwan, his legacy would be that Chinese national interests would prevail over Communist and Socialist rhetoric. What was best for the people was all that really counted. Under Deng, peasants' standard of living improved more than at any time in China's history. Longtime followers of Asian affairs Todd Crowell and Thomas Hon Wing Polin assess his stature in world history: "Deng lifted more people out of poverty than any other world leader, anytime, anywhere."[38]

Jiang Zemin and Party Reform 4

Deng Xiaoping died in February 1997, but his successor, Jiang Zemin, continued his policy of slowly introducing capitalism into China's economy. Like his mentor, Jiang argued that only the social stability offered by a strong single political party could allow China to achieve economic well-being. Jiang, and most CCP leaders, believe that political freedom in China must evolve in cautious, carefully tested steps. The people must be trained from the village level up over several generations before the government can risk holding free national elections.

For Jiang and the rest of China's leaders, the problem is that as people experience economic freedom, they also seek a voice in national policy making. C.H. Kwan, a visiting scholar at the Brookings Institution, writes,

> The demand for democracy has been increasing along with incomes, however, while the reputation of the Communist Party has been badly hurt by widespread corruption among government officials and a rising crime rate. The "policy mix" of economic liberalization and political dictatorship has reached its limit; the Communist Party needs to reform itself or it will face grave consequences.[39]

Jiang's Reform Program: The National Fifteenth Party Congress

Although Jiang already held the major power positions in the party and the government, he had to stay in the background while Deng was alive. When the ninety-two-year-old Deng died, many expected Jiang to fade away and a more assertive leader to emerge. But Jiang quickly shed his reputation as a lightweight politician and took control at the Fifteenth National Party Congress in 1997. Jiang guided the Party Congress with political cunning, forcing his main rival on the Standing Committee, Qiao Shi, into retirement and positioning his economic adviser, Zhu Rongji, for the premiership. As for his economic policies, Jiang met no serious opposition.

Jiang realized, however, that China's legal system was unsuitable for regulating China's budding business economy. Traditionally, the Chinese had settled disputes without resorting to legal codes and courts. Confucian principles declared that group and peer pressure from the family, neighborhood, and workplace should guarantee that people would conduct themselves virtuously. However, late–twentieth-century China had been transformed into a capitalist type of economy where such principles were seen by potential investors as inadequate protection of their interests.

Jiang Zemin succeeded Deng Xiaoping in 1997.

Chinese leaders understand that to attract more foreign investment they must establish a strong legal system that protects ownership rights to property. The concept of property necessarily includes both material goods and intellectual ideas. Furthermore, in the past, investors were discouraged by the pervasive system of political corruption. However, officials realize they must demonstrate that they are tackling the more blatant abuses of power. In March 1998 Jiang proposed a large number of legal reforms. As Andy Xie, the Greater China economist at Morgan Stanley Dean Witter in Hong Kong, explains, "The modernization of the mainland is essentially a process through which the country fights against its past to establish a new order based on the rule of law."[40]

Preserving Social Order

In all his efforts at reform, Jiang has to deal with resistance from some members of the Communist Party. Opponents of Jiang's program point to increased social unrest as evidence that eco-

The Scholar-Statesman

Jiang Zemin is the first Communist Chinese leader with a university education. An engineer by training, Jiang published several technical articles on electronic information technology. His intellect is not one-dimensional, however. He speaks several languages, including English, Russian, and Romanian. He is also well versed in literature. He can quote in English the "To be or not to be" soliloquy from Shakespeare's *Hamlet* and Percy Bysshe Shelley's poem "Ode to the West Wind." When visiting Russia, Jiang impressed his hosts with his scholarly analysis of Leo Tolstoy's novels. In his spare time he plays classical Chinese erhu (a type of fiddle), the flute, and the piano.

Close friends call Jiang a scholar-statesman. Indeed, he is well acquainted with some of the most important political documents in the world.

In December 1986, Shanghai students at Jiang's alma mater, Jiaotong University, had organized demonstrations calling for more political freedoms in wake of activist Fang Lizhi's fiery speeches for democracy. As mayor of Shanghai, Jiang took on the responsibility of defusing the students' protests. He met with three thousand students at the university on December 18 and called for calm and order. Students answered with phrases from the U.S. Declaration of Independence. *Time* journalist Jaime Florcruz writes in the article "Long Live the Students" that "Jiang glibly recited entire sections of the Declaration—in English—and wondered whether the students really grasped the spirit of the document." He then "lectured them on the need for order, arguing 'there is no absolute freedom anywhere in the world.'"

nomic reform will not work. Still, within the party some realize that complaints among the people that officials get rich while the peasants and low-income workers struggle to make ends meet, have some validity. In 2001 the CCP published a three-hundred-page report citing widespread popular discontent with party corruption and a stagnant rural income as potential sparks for a general rural uprising in the future.

Violence has already been an occasional problem in the countryside. Armed only with farm hoes and other common implements, villagers and peasants have at one time or another attacked government and party officials in almost every province. In 1997 alone, according to *Washington Post* correspondent Andy Kennedy, the government admitted "that there were more than 10,000 'unruly incidents' by farmers." These incidents ranged from the innocent—"filing petitions"—to the dangerous—"attempting to destroy government offices."[41] Some incidents have been particularly violent. In August 2000, for example, ten thousand farmers in the Jiangxi province burned police cars and attacked government offices when local officials suppressed information from Beijing about taxes. And in the Liaoling province in northeast China, twenty thousand people rioted for three days in February 2000, protesting the layoffs resulting from the privatization of the local molybdenum mine. The army finally had to be called in to restore order.

Such incidents naturally alarm authorities. The concept of disorder, says historian Francesco Sisci, derives from the Chinese word *luan*, which implied "total chaos . . . a situation in which people did not have enough to eat or to wear, or a shelter, and were threatened by military destruction, so their very survival was at stake."[42] Although the support of the urban population is important, the party is most concerned with discontent in rural China. Jiang told a group of top party officials in 2001 that "rural stability is key to the stability of the entire nation."[43]

Reviving the CCP

In a more general sense, Jiang believes that China's problem is a spiritual one. Although the CCP might be seen as a means of attaining privileges and economic opportunities, it is no longer a spiritual guide for most Chinese. The strong sense of social duty that brought people together early in the Mao era disappeared with Deng's reforms. Young Chinese raised during the 1980s know nothing of their parents' and grandparents' sacrifices and struggles to build China. This uprooting of values affects everyone. Economic reform may fill the pocketbook, but it seems to leave a void in people's spirit. *Time Asia* journalist Terry McCarthy describes the spiritual dilemma for the younger generations of Chinese today:

> Accompanying this enormous change is an equally momentous loss of innocence, an awakening to the harshness of life in a free-market system. What does it mean to be happy in China today? Young people have no model to follow: all their parents taught them was to make as much money as they could, as quickly as they could. Spiritually China is a void; religion is a distant concept to most young Chinese, and they have found little with which to replace it. Contemporary Chinese works of art and literature are shot through with cynicism and a dash of despair at the all-embracing materialism they see everywhere around them.[44]

Many people attribute the appeal of the movement known as Falun Gong and the revival of religion in China to this spiritual crisis. Journalist Jaime A. Florcruz of *Time Asia* writes that people in China are searching for "comfort and security—and meaning—to their lives."[45] China watchers say that if the Communist Party is seen merely as a vehicle for material success, then it can never fill this human need for spiritual guidance. Once economic prosperity has spread throughout China, the people will still be looking for a spiritual anchor.

Party leaders have acknowledged this crisis of spirit. Jiang initiated a drive to revive traditional Chinese values to fill this spiritual void. As CNN China correspondent Willy Wo-Lap Lam writes, "A source close to the president's camp said he wanted

Falun Gong

A child practices Falun Gong, an outlawed spiritual meditation program.

Until April 1999 Falun Gong was registered with the State Sports Administration. It blends teachings from Buddhism and Taoism with a traditional meditation exercise program from the martial art of qigong. Today, the CCP has outlawed Falun Gong as an evil cult teaching superstitions and endangering lives of the Chinese people. The number of followers is estimated to be between 40 and 70 million. The government claims that Falun Gong has about 40 million followers.

In his article "Falungong: Part 2: A Rude Awakening," scholar Francesco Sisci explains what hard-liners like Jiang Zemin saw as threatening about Falun Gong:

> What was so important about being a religion rather than just a sport association? The official label did not make any difference to its spiritual practices, so, arguably, the issue was not about religion but about power. . . . In fact the Falungong agenda looked [to hard-liners] quite political. The sect was against modern Western science, preached the end of the world, forbade its followers watching TV or being treated in hospitals, and maintained that diseases do not exist and that ailments are due to sins people commit. . . . A Falungong follower who does not watch TV is not influenced by government propaganda, and by entrusting his own health to the sect rather than to public hospitals, he cedes all his person to the sect.

a resuscitation of values dear to Confucius such as benevolence, respect for elders, and contentment with one's station in life. Jiang is impressed by how traditional virtues have been a stabilizing factor in Asian countries influenced by Confucius such as Japan, South Korea, and in particular, Singapore."[46] By connecting the Communist Party to these traditional values, Jiang hopes to silence criticism of the party. Unlike Mao, who attacked China's Confucian culture as feudal, Jiang sees an opportunity for the party to appeal to national pride by linking itself to China's past. The party, Jiang contends, is part of China's evolutionary progress, and it is prepared to build China into a world power. Therefore, the people should trust the party.

Scientific Marxism

China's leaders are asking the people to be patient. Jiang has said that it will take a hundred years before China's economy can be described as developed. And then, according to Yan Shuhan, an official at the influential Central Party School in Beijing, Jiang believes that "socialism and the entire process of maturity towards communism will take another 10–20 generations. It's only then that China can enter the early stages of communism, and it will take another 10–20 generations before true communism can be attained. Communism is still our ultimate objective as a Party, but it may take several thousand years."[47] Jiang says this philosophy, which he calls scientific Marxism, demands flexibility. He told senior military officers in 2001 that Marxism requires two principles: ideological emancipation and seeking truth from facts. According to Jiang, "The two principles serve as the touchstone which tests whether we are real Marxists. . . . We should take a scientific attitude by viewing Marxism as a science that develops along with the development of the reality."[48]

The Pace of Political Reform

Although governments around the world welcome China's economic progress, they continue to condemn China for suppressing the voices of democracy. Many critics insist that the freedom

The Anticorruption Campaign

China's leaders have made cleaning up corruption a high priority, but because most positions of responsibility are held by CCP members, rooting out corruption in government will mean cleaning up the party itself. In 2001 some of the people convicted and punished included top bank officials, a vice minister of public security, the mayor of Senyang City and his assistant, a provincial governor, dozens of CCP officials, bank directors, and dozens of CCP cadres.

A *People's Daily* article, "Chinese Prosecutors Uncover Seventeen Hundred Corrupt Officials," describes the extent of the government's efforts in just a six-month period in 2001: "China's top prosecutor Han Zhubin [procurator general of the Supreme People's Court] said . . . that during the January–June period, Chinese prosecutors nationwide uncovered 25,073 cases of white-collar crime, involving 27,793 Party and government employees, of which 1,781 were above the county-head level."

to exchange ideas and to take risks without government interference is a precondition to continued growth in China. Therefore, they conclude, China must initiate political freedoms now or the economy will decline, leading to widespread social disorder. If this were to happen, these critics argue, the Deng-Jiang economic reforms would be discredited and abandoned. The result would be a PLA move to restore order, followed by a restoration of hard-line Mao-era supervision of people's lives and state ownership of the economy.

Other analysts conclude that China is on the right track. They maintain that political freedom is meaningless to peasants and workers who lack adequate food and shelter. These "economy-first" analysts contend that only when the majority of people have attained middle-class comfort will they care about political freedom. For now, these analysts believe, social stability and a step-by-step evolution toward more freedoms is the only workable plan. This school of thought is represented not just by the mainstream Chinese Communist Party leaders but also by much of the business world in the West.

Capitalists Are Communists Too

As China changes, so does the CCP. Some observers believe that ultimately there may be no distinction between capitalists and Communists. In a September 7, 2001, interview with *Asiaweek*, Yan Shuhan, an official at the Central Party School in Beijing, offers the Communist Party's justification for recruiting private business people:

> There are now six new classes of people that did not exist before the start of market reforms in 1978, and it is important that the most outstanding among them be invited to join the Party—private enterprise managers, private enterprise owners, small businessmen and women, white-collar professionals, individual contractors, and other professionals working in private capacities. They are not the same exploiters of the masses as those before the 1949 liberation. They grew rich under the Party's socialist market reforms. They are a reflection of modern China.

The paradox for Jiang is that achieving the kind of true communism he envisions may require a loosening of the party's hold on power. Analyzing a December 1999 poll of fifty top Chinese researchers, sociologist Lu Jianhua of the Chinese Academy of Social Sciences (CASS) wrote that:

> This poll shows the experts put lagging political reform as the biggest constraint China faces in the first decade of the new [twenty-first] century. The experts apparently expect that political reform can lead to the melioration of solution of China's most serious problems. Political reform is very important for putting the entire society on track for healthier development.[49]

Freedom of Speech

Although the suppression of dissent gets headlines in the foreign press, close observers of China today report that the state is interfering less in people's lives than in any time in recent memory. As long as people confine their comments to economic issues, China's leaders generally tolerate criticism. Journalist Zhang Li-Fen of the BBC describes conditions in China today:

"People have more freedom and scope for basic choices in their lives than ever before—as long as they do not openly challenge the Party and its legitimacy."[50] If the government senses a challenge to the CCP's authority, however, it reverts to its authoritarian past. Officials invoke Article 105 of the 1997 penal code, which calls for detention or arrest of "those involved in organizing, scheming or acting to subvert the political power of the state and overthrow the socialist system."[51]

Among the most scrutinized people in China are journalists. The government owns and supervises all news media, and it can be difficult for journalists to report events objectively. In an interview with correspondent Mike Wallace of CBS in September 2000, Jiang responded to criticism of media restrictions, saying, "Freedom of the press should be subordinate to the interests of the nation. How can you allow such freedom to damage the national interests?" One major challenge to the government's control of information has been the Internet. Jiang told Wallace that the government would continue to selectively ban foreign news sites: "We need to be selective. We hope to restrict as much as possible information not conducive to China's development."[52]

Party membership offers no immunity to pressure. Members who dare step out of line to express opposing views risk their positions. In what is called the Spring Crackdown of 2000, Jiang attacked CCP members for "openly expressing opposition to the party line in newspapers, books, and speeches."[53] The purge of intellectuals that followed was triggered by an essay criticizing China's extravagance in celebrating fifty years of Communist rule. The author, Li Shenzhi, a highly respected academic at CASS, was fired. In the following months, more than two dozen editors, publishers, and writers were demoted or dismissed from their positions for being somehow connected with critical pieces about the government, widespread corruption, and social problems.

Such actions are perfectly legal under China's constitution. Although the Chinese constitution guarantees freedom of speech, its preamble states that "under the leadership of the Communist

Party of China and the guidance of Marxist-Leninism and Mao Zedong Thought, the Chinese people of all nationalities shall continue to adhere to the people's democratic dictatorship and follow the socialist road."[54] Any challenge to the leadership is therefore a violation of the basic framework of Chinese law.

Similarly, any challenge to the primacy of the Communist Party is illegal. The constitution guarantees multiple political parties, but only those that submit to the guidance of the CCP. Thousands of Chinese have been jailed because they argue for competing political parties. Furthermore, whether or not someone's actions violate the constitution often never comes up because in many cases there is no trial. Another loophole in the legal system still allows the government to detain persons without trial and to sentence them to three years of "reeducation-through-labor"—essentially forced labor camps. The U.S. Department of State reports that in 1997 "there were some 230,000 persons in reeducation-through-labor camps."[55]

Women watch a video in a correctional facility aimed at breaking their alliance to Falun Gong.

Publishing and Profits

Counterbalancing the drive to control information is the fact that China's leaders are pushing state-run media to become self-supporting. As a result, the rules of the marketplace prevail. A senior associate at the Carnegie Endowment for International Peace, Pei Minxin, explains:

> As market forces have fundamentally altered the structures and practices of the Chinese print media, Chinese publishing houses are now driven primarily by profit motives and have become willing to take more political risks. In the meantime, the explosive growth of the media market has overtaxed the capacity of the official censors, forcing the government to curtail its control.[56]

The government can still censor or ban works and discipline artists and publishers officially, but public demand seems to be more important than censorship in determining what gets published. The people are drawn to popular culture, preferring to be entertained with stories of sex, adultery, adventure, government abuse of power, and family strife.

In-house censors, representatives of the CCP who work in the approximately five hundred government-approved publishing houses, allow most manuscripts to be published. Once something is published, the government's official censors, the State Publications Administration and Party Propaganda Bureau, determine what continues in circulation. The problem for the government is usually that by pulling a book off store shelves, the government makes that book much more popular. Howard Goldblatt, who teaches Chinese at the University of Colorado at Boulder, explains that when popular author Mo Yan's books "*The Republic of Wine* and *Big Breasts and Wide Hips* were ordered pulled from the shelves, hundreds of thousands of pirated copies . . . [appeared] in bookstalls across China."[57]

Government censors rarely intervene unless a work is blatantly pornographic, but sometimes books depicting young Chinese spiritually adrift and escaping into sex and drugs draw

Press Censorship: The "Seven Nos"

In an article titled "China: Government Issues New List of Banned Media Topics," the Committee to Protect Journalists (CPJ), an international organization based in New York City, criticized the Chinese government for one of its more recent crackdowns on press freedom in China. The "Seven Nos" guideline was communicated to editors in January 2001, but the government withheld publication of the guidelines until August 2001.

The new policy bans all press reports that:

1. Negate the guiding role of Marxism, Mao Zedong Thought, or Deng Xiaoping Theory;
2. Oppose the guiding principles, official line, or policies of the Communist Party;
3. Reveal state secrets, damage national security, or harm national interests;
4. Oppose official policies regarding minority nationalities and religion, or harm national unity and affect social stability;
5. Advocate murder, violence, obscenity, superstition, or pseudo-science;
6. Spread rumors or falsified news, or interfere in the work of the party and government;
7. Violate party propaganda discipline, or national publishing and advertising regulations.

government censorship. Two young writers, Mian Mian and Wei Hui, who are described by *Time Asia* magazine as "vying for recognition as China's 'bad girl of letters,'" had recent novels banned because they depicted "steamy . . . sex, drugs and dropout chic."[58] What will get censored is, however, difficult for Chinese journalists to determine in advance. A producer at Central China Television (CCTV), the national television network, describes trying to determine topics the government will censor as "a game. You never know how far you can go unless a leader gives you a sign."[59]

Broadcasting Media

Overall, however, China's mass media are controlled by the same market forces that operate in nations that do not practice censorship. CCTV, the state-owned national network, must operate as if it were a private corporation. The network makes money by selling advertisers airtime, and advertisers want to appeal to the largest audience. Therefore, the network's programs are largely determined by the viewers' tastes. According to China specialist Allison Liu Jernow, because the viewers want popular culture more than politics and history, there is a "rise of lightweight and sensational news, popular but politically unthreatening."[60] Consumers prefer stories about self-improvement, enhancing their sex life, or finding dates.

This fondness for popular culture rather than hard political stories is reflected in the programming on China's television and radio stations. With the party's blessing, CCTV is producing more sensational exposés on crime and corruption. Late-night radio call-in shows that answer questions about people's sex lives draw tens of thousands of listeners from all over China. In any case, government control of television and radio is often moot since satellite and cable programs from outside China already are beamed to Guangdong province in southern China.

The Internet

Maintaining control over what amounts to a gigantic media empire is an almost impossible task. Trying to control what is broadcast over the Internet by hundreds of millions of individuals and organizations is even more daunting. Some observers believe the Internet may end up breaking the CCP's grip on China altogether. Guo Liang of CASS explains in an allusion to Mao's declaration that "to have power you need two things: the gun and the pen." Today, Guo says, "the Communist Party has the gun, but the Internet is now the pen."[61]

Chinese authorities do what they can to control the Internet, limiting what is available on the Internet from outside China, who uses the worldwide web, who offers websites and their content, and who provides Internet service in China. According to government regulations, Internet service providers must keep records of "the time of . . . subscribers' access to the Internet, the subscribers' account numbers, the addresses or domain names of the Web sites, and the main telephone numbers they use."[62] Those who provide content on the web must keep records of everything posted on their sites. Internet service providers, meanwhile, are required to maintain logs of all information posted on their sites. Hundreds of violators are punished annually, but rather than discouraging violations, enforcement seems only to be leading more people to defy the authorities. For every online bulletin board or chat room that is shut down, several new ones open.

Even with government monitoring, most of China's 33 million users feel liberated by the Internet. A Beijing University student says that "the atmosphere . . . on the Internet is far more free than the atmosphere in our country generally. When you are in front of a computer no one can control your soul or your spirit."[63] One reason attempts to control the Internet have failed is that users simply find alternative routes to information whenever the government blocks websites.

In China, the government strictly regulates what is broadcast over the Internet and service providers must keep detailed records of subscribers' activities.

In 1987, China established elections to choose village committee members and village heads.

The Roots of Democracy

Even as the party tries to control the flow of information, the roots of democracy are spreading in villages throughout China—often with the party's blessing. In 1987 China passed a law establishing elections to choose village committee members and village heads. By instituting elections at the village level, party leaders hope that "more honest, popular, and reform-minded leaders [will get] into positions of local power . . . thus forestalling dissent,"[64] according to Anne F. Thurston, a member of the Carter Center of Atlanta, a nonprofit organization dedicated to fostering free and fair elections around the world.

In most of the nearly 1 million villages across China, multiple-candidate elections have been held. Once elected, the officials serve three-year terms. According to the head of the Carter Center team, Robert Pastor, "China's village elections are a significant and positive development in empowering China's 900 million farmers."[65] Often, elected members and chiefs are not members of the party, although they usually join after election. Today about seven out of ten village chiefs are members of the party.

Free elections at higher governmental levels have also been held. In 2001, for example, cities such as Shanghai, Nanjing, and Hangzhou began holding community council elections, a move seen by many as further proof that the CCP intends to expand grassroots democracy. Elections have also been held in cities such as Shenzhen and Qingdao, although these have not been officially authorized by top party officials in Beijing. On the other hand, these officials have not obstructed elections either. By allowing such unauthorized elections to go forward, party officials can analyze the results and, if they like what they see, they can then officially extend democratic reforms.

These reforms, modest as they might be, follow China's traditional approach of changing slowly, but they illustrate that the party is responsive to the people's wishes. As Zhao Suisheng, program director at the Center for China-U.S. Cooperation at the University of Denver, writes about democratic reform in China's future,

> The transition would come from above and a democratic society could begin to develop gradually under the Communist state.
>
> Unless the CCP were totally devastated by such a transition, which is unlikely, it would probably be in the best position to win elections. The party's organizational sophistication and control over resources would give it enormous advantages and probably enable it to win elections.
>
> In this case, the CCP would continue to be a ruling party, and a democratized China could have a system like those in Taiwan and Japan, where a single party dominates.[66]

If the practice of elections continues to develop, the next generation of Communist leaders may preside over a transition to some form of provincial or national elections. The real issue for the next generation of leaders—referred to as the fourth generation of leaders—will be how to prepare the country for even more sweeping changes. Managing change will be made all the more difficult by some of China's other current social problems as well as by challenges from abroad.

China's Future: The New Generation

5

China entered the twenty-first century possessed of enormous potential but faced with many challenges. The fourth generation of leaders likely will give way to a so-called fifth generation, born during the 1950s and early 1960s, after 2010. Now in their forties and fifties, potential leaders entered the 1980s with little commitment to any ideology except Deng Xiaoping's slogan, "To get rich is glorious."[67]

The Under-Forty Generation

Lined up behind the fifth generation is an even more diverse generation of Chinese born since the mid-1970s. There are 630 million people in China under forty years old, making up more than half the country's population. During their lifetime, China has changed more than almost any other society in history. Author Terry McCarthy writes, "The country looks nothing like the battered, colorless society that emerged from the ruins of the Cultural Revolution. An entirely new economic and social landscape has been created."[68] Those born during the late seventies and early eighties are sometimes referred to as the Deng generation because their values were formed as China veered right economically. Fast on their heels came the so-called wired generation, those born during the late eighties and early nineties who are becoming regular Internet users. Lisa Movius, a writer living in Shanghai, describes them as "better educated, more culturally aware, more ambitious, more Western in tastes and sensibilities, more open to new ideas and—influenced perhaps by post–Cultural Revolution cynicism—resolutely indifferent to both authority and ideology."[69]

The young people of China, dubbed the wired generation, have become regular Internet users.

In fact, cataloging differences among Chinese according to generations is becoming almost impossible. Tony Zhang, founder of the popular bilingual entertainment website China Now, writes that "things are changing so quickly, a new generation gap emerges every three to four years."[70] Movius explains that urbanites aged eighteen to thirty-five encompass at least three distinct generations, with vastly different sensibilities and tastes: "the 30-something Cultural Revolution babies, the 25- to 30-year-old reform era generation and the under-25 post-reform group, those brassily demanding 'little emperors.'"[71] Complicating the picture of modern China is the large number of the thirty- and forty-year-olds who are simply devoted to creating and expanding China's business culture.

Traditional Values and Change

As these worldly and increasingly westernized younger people grow older, Chinese culture is undergoing profound change. Using the analogy of the Great Wall, built in ancient times to protect China from foreign invasions, sociologists Godwin Chu and

Yanan Ju conclude that China risks losing its identity: "[The] Great Wall is crumbling. It seems to lie in ruins, waiting for a modern miracle to resurrect it and imbue new life to the Chinese society it has traditionally defended."[72] Chu and Ju consider these changes to be part of a dangerous trend. They write that the traditional values have declined, and that twenty-five years of Maoism have left the people without their cultural anchor.

Chinese social philosophy has always taught that individual rights and privacy must be subordinate to group values. To the Chinese, the Western concept of individualism is considered selfish and self-centered. But Western influence is changing Chinese values. In a survey, Chu and Ju measured individualism and collectivism as personal values in China. They report that the more that respondents were exposed to Western culture, the more likely they selected the response "the most important thing in one's life is to live happily" over the other choice, "the most important thing in one's life is to make some contributions

A boy wears a mask to avoid breathing fumes. China is home to seven of the ten most polluted cities in the world.

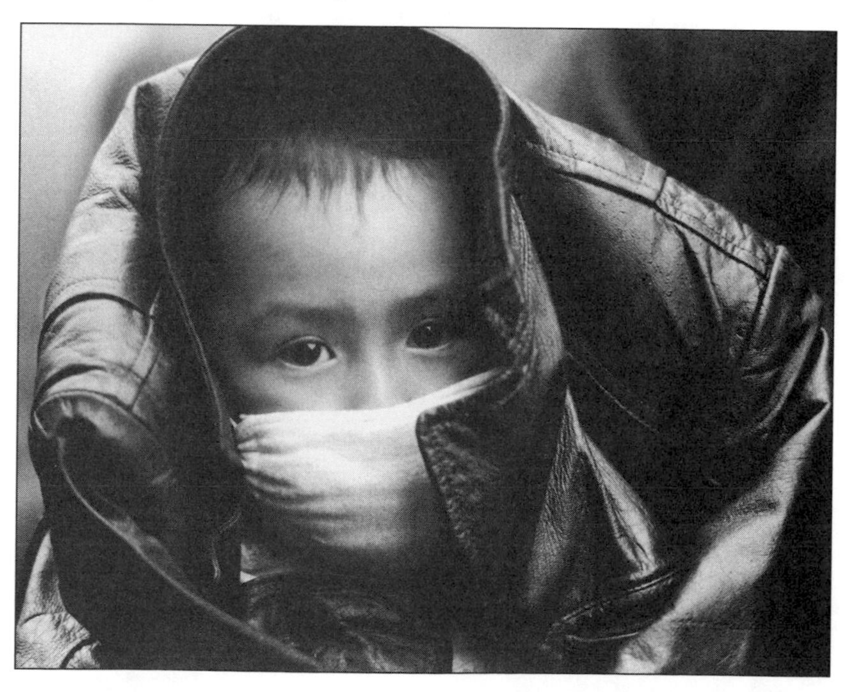

Environmental Problems

Typically, China never worried much about environmental issues as it struggled to feed and house a billion people. But the transition to a market economy has brought gigantic environmental problems. The government recognizes that soon environmental issues will outweigh all other problems. Without radical changes in soil, energy, and water use, large sections of populated China will become mostly uninhabitable.

Currently, China is home to seven of the ten most polluted cities in the world. Much of the pollution comes from the heavy use of low-grade coal, which is still increasing rapidly. According to a United Nations Development Programme (UNDP) report, titled "Urban and Rural Pollution: Urban Air Pollution," "Only 26 percent of the coal produced in China is successfully converted to energy; the rest is wasted." The report claims that "the air quality in more than 500 major Chinese cities is below WHO's [the World Health Organization] criteria."

The UNDP says that 81.6 percent of the cities in China have problems with acid rain. The problems include a

> high level of sulfur dioxide emissions from fossil fuel combustion. . . . In addition, nitrogen oxide is contributing to acid rain in 88 major Chinese cities. . . . The total area affected by acid rain in China now accounts for 29 percent of the nation's total territory. The affected areas are mainly concentrated in the Southern Yangtze area, the Sichuan Basin and the areas east of the Qinghai-Tibet Plateau. The most polluted cities for nitrogen oxide are Beijing, Guangzhou, Urumqi and Anshan.

In early 2002 China started an $84-billion program to fight pollution. According to an article on the CNN website titled "China Steps Up Pollution War," the government "hopes to have reduced the total amount of pollutants in the air, water and soil by 10 percent of 2000 levels. The plan will focus on reducing air and water pollution, and cleaning up heavily polluted rivers, lakes and seas."

The CNN article also quotes Xie Zhenhua, director of the State Environmental Protection Administration, as saying, "Never has the Chinese government put the environment issue in such an important position. It is vital to stability and prosperity of our country and people." Any additional expenses will be picked up by local governments and businesses guilty of polluting.

Traditionally, the eldest male of the family was expected to house and care for his parents in their old age. This custom is slowly disappearing as many people move from small family oriented villages to cities.

to society." And young people "were about five times as likely as old people" to respond this way.[73]

One of the oldest Confucian values is showing respect and caring for one's elders. In the past, the oldest male child was expected to house and care for his parents in their old age. Today, this custom is still maintained in the countryside, but in the cities, the elderly frequently live on their own or in retirement homes. Sociologist Li Baoliang, who has studied the conditions of senior citizens in China, concludes, "Often . . . [senior citizens] don't get enough care from their children and psychologically they don't get enough support, so they leave home to live at an old people's home."[74]

On the job, young professionals are beginning to assert themselves in ways that traditional Chinese culture would have condemned. They speak out more and even argue with older workers with whom they disagree. They do not fear authority the way their parents' generation did. And age is no longer considered a criterion for leadership. Chu and Ju discovered that out of eleven qualities, seniority was considered an important quality by only 1.2 percent of the respondents. Seniority was also ranked last by those surveyed as an important promotion criteria. Even middle-aged Chinese workers have less respect for seniority as the major qualification for advancement. Bad experiences under the former communal and collective systems have convinced them that talent should be the criteria for success, not seniority.

Another value that illustrates the impact of Western culture on China is how much more openly younger people display romantic feelings. Although Chinese literature is full of love stories, the reality of arranged marriages and restricted contact between males and females meant that young men and women had to suppress their romantic feelings. Today, however, teenagers talk about and express their romantic feelings, even in public. Junior English majors at Capital Normal University in Beijing conducted extensive surveys about contemporary life in China. One participant, Zhang Wei, describes the relationships between young men and women: "Today, influenced by [Western] culture, young lovers become very open. It's often seen in public place that sweet lovers embrace or kiss each other."[75]

Marriage and the Family

Another traditional value, the old-fashioned model of the close-knit family, still prevails, but relatively rare is the household in which three or four generations live under the same roof. In urban areas especially, such extended families are uncommon, except for homes in which the immediate parents might live with married children. The Confucian idea that children should be respectful and loyal to their parents is still popular; however, the younger the parents, the more likely they are to tolerate their children talking back, a sign of independence and disobedience that was not tolerated in the past.

Working to reduce family cohesion is the government policy of discouraging parents from having more than one child. Whereas in the past Chinese families tended to be large, now one

Unlike the culture of their elders, young people today are open with their feelings and affectionate with one another in public.

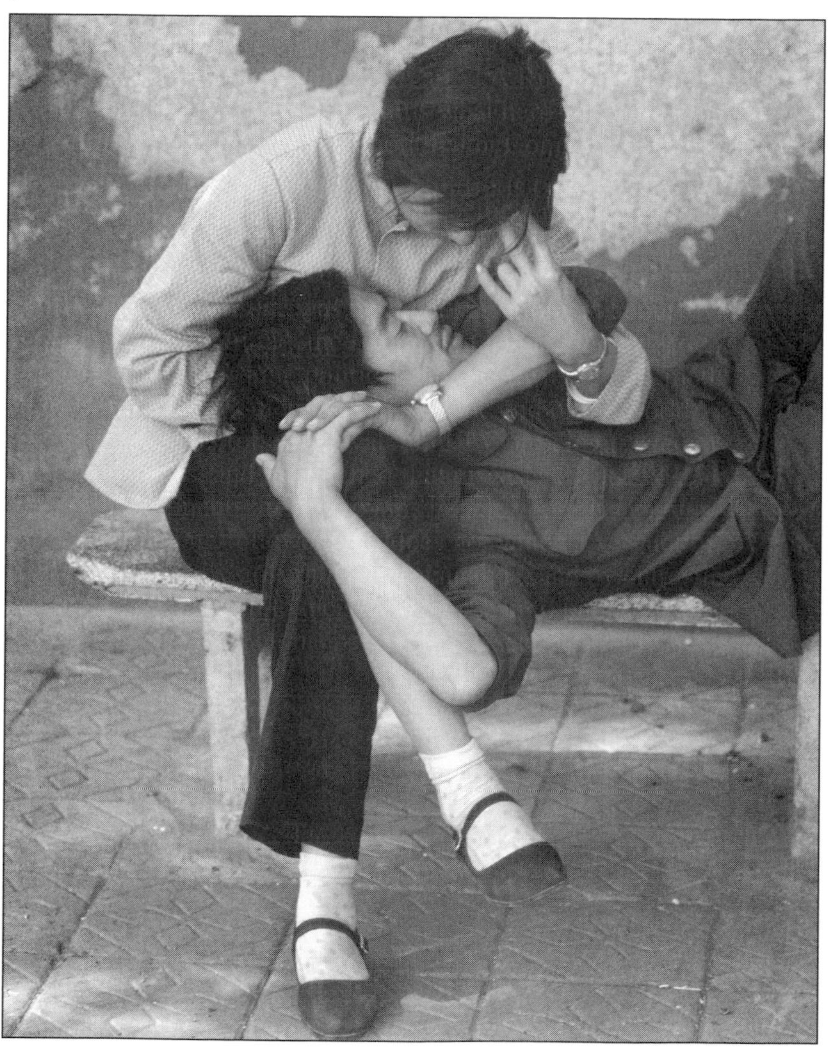

child is the norm—at least in the cities. In fact, today many couples are choosing not to have children at all. Xia Meng, who participated in the Capital Normal University surveys, explains that "the DINK (double income no kids) family is fashionable, which could not be accepted in the traditional Chinese convention. The DINK couples are mainly from well-educated people with a bigger income. They care more about careers instead of children."[76] The numbers of such households may be small, but in the larger cities DINK couples freely express their intention not to have children. Before the 1990s such couples would have been outcasts because they were seen as disloyal to Chinese traditions.

Other traditions in family life are also falling by the wayside. Whereas in the past women tended to marry young, the marriage age is increasing, at least in the cities, as young women set their sights more on careers than ever before. With more couples delaying marriage, China's urban population is experiencing a sexual revolution. More and more young adults have premarital sex. A majority of sixty-five hundred Chinese men and women between fourteen and twenty-eight years of age responding to a survey indicated that they are "comfortable with the idea of pre-marital sex."[77] It is not uncommon for a young couple to live together without getting married.

Some traditions remain strong or are even undergoing a revival. For example, the old custom of men having mistresses is gaining in popularity. Yan Li, a correspondent with the *People's Daily*, observes that "it has been rampant in some developed provinces in recent years that people cohabitate with a person other than his spouse, regarding this woman as the 'second wife.'" In response to the rise in this practice, China has revised its laws to make adultery illegal and has declared that property and wages gained by either party in a marriage are held jointly. Yan writes that if the parties undergoing a divorce cannot agree to a division of property, "the people's court will make decisions in favor of the offspring and the female."[78]

Such protections for women are part of a larger social trend in China in which women have slowly moved into leadership positions at most levels of government. For example, in 2000, 22 percent of the almost three thousand delegates to the National People's Congress (NPC) were women. Women are also active in provincial, prefecture, and county levels of the party. More than four hundred of China's four thousand mayors are women; hundreds more serve as vice mayors, and more are serving as governors or vice governors in almost all of China's provinces, municipalities, and autonomous regions.

However, women have less influence within the CCP itself. In the powerful party Standing Committee, for example, all seven members are men, and none of the fifteen full Politburo members are women. Of the top twenty-five persons in the CCP, only one is a woman, Wu Yi, a delegate to the NPC.

Materialism

The traditional value of working hard is still widely held, and it is expressed more than ever in the younger generation's seeming obsession with making money. China specialist Geremie R. Barme describes this attitude as "Consumerism. Computers. Cash. The three C's seem to define today's urban Chinese youth."[79] Sharon Hu, a twenty-two-year-old university student in 2001, explained to an interviewer, "We are not like those students in 1989 [the Tiananmen Square pro-democracy demonstrators]. We are more interested in an economic revolution. And, you know, I don't think in China today there is that much difference between Communism and capitalism."[80]

Hu's comment is one more emblem of the fact that fewer Chinese need the backing of the Communist Party to prosper. The government's endorsement of private enterprise allows the new middle class to play a key role in the economic life of the nation independent of the party. This economic independence translates into greater influence by ordinary Chinese over political affairs. BBC correspondent Zhang Li-Fen explains that "they [the middle class] have become opinion formers on issues of public concern and set trends in civic and cultural life, from tourism and the arts to sex education. . . . They are contributing to the formation of a civil society in China."[81]

China Makes the *Fortune* Five-Hundred List

For the first time since the Communists took over, Chinese businesses are being recognized as among the larger companies in the world. *Fortune* magazine listed twelve Chinese companies among the top five hundred companies in the world for 2000. Three of them were in the top one hundred.

In his article "Fortune Global Five Hundred: The World's Largest Corporations," *Fortune* magazine correspondent Jeremy Kahn writes about China's "emergence as an economic powerhouse":

> The number of Chinese businesses on the list continues to expand as more and more corporations have their books audited according to Western standards. This year 12 Chinese companies made the list—in industries from banking to telecommunications—two more than last year. China's new entrants include China Mobile (No. 336), a state-owned phone company with $15 billion in sales, and China National Petroleum (No. 83), a state-owned energy company that racked up $42 billion in sales and is the Global 500's largest employer, with a payroll of 1,292,558.

Correcting the Brain Drain

Interestingly, many who are contributing to a better society are Chinese who are returning after earning university degrees in the West. In the past most students stayed in Europe and the United States to work after they graduated. Since the late 1990s, however, government offers of low-interest loans and tax breaks to overseas students who return to China has begun to correct what has been a "brain drain."

Business graduates were the first to return, attracted by the opportunities posed by a Chinese market of more than a billion consumers. Then came those with computer science degrees anxious to be part of China's drive to build state-of-the-art computer networks. Now the government has begun attracting young scientists with advanced degrees to return home to work in twenty-six specially built "pioneering parks" located on the outskirts of Beijing, Shanghai, and Guangzhou. More than a thousand companies have started up at these high-tech parks since 1996. Government tax subsidies and other financial breaks allow these companies to attract Western-educated employees with higher salaries and new laboratories with clean, up-to-date equipment.

Chinese overseas graduates are returning because of the positive reputation of these high-tech companies. And as Hannah Beech of *Time Asia* explains, they are motivated both by self-interest and patriotism: "'No matter how talented we are, there's a feeling that being Chinese limits our success in America,' says Hu Songnian, 31, who studied genetics at the University of Washington. 'I would rather work in China, where I can help my country and have my work be appreciated.'"[82]

No matter what other motives are at work in China, patriotism has not disappeared. Whenever conflicts arise with other nations, the Chinese are quick to voice support for their country. For example, when the United States mistakenly bombed the Chinese embassy in Belgrade, Yugoslavia, on May 8, 1999, killing three Chinese employees, hundreds of thousands of protesters took to the streets in cities across China. They returned to the streets in 2001 in anger when an American spy plane and a Chinese fighter had a midair collision in April 2001, resulting in the death of the fighter's pilot.

China's Relations with the United States

The spy plane incident threw into sharp relief how complex China's relationship with the United States is. When Mao Zedong ruled China, he wanted to avoid being dependent on foreigners for economic growth. He had visions of China leading the poorer world nations in an alliance that would remain free of ties to the United States and the Soviet Union. However, Mao eventually concluded that China needed American assistance to build its economy. Thus, during the 1970s Mao allowed Zhou Enlai to initiate formal diplomatic talks that led to official recognition of the People's Republic of China by the United States. Ever since, the two nations have had friendly, although sometimes tense, relations.

Some of those tensions have been the result of China's backing of regimes unfriendly to the United States, such as Iran and North Korea. Today, Chinese officials realize that China can continue its economic development only in a peaceful world environment. As a result, they have withdrawn support of most radical regimes around the globe. After terrorists destroyed New York's World Trade Towers on September 11, 2001, for example, China joined with the United States not only to condemn the terrorists but also to share sensitive intelligence about terrorist training camps in Afghanistan, which shares a border with China's Xinjiang autonomous province. Such cooperation also served Chinese interests since thousands of Mus-

Protesters react to the crash of a Chinese fighter plane with an American spy plane by protesting American invasion of their airspace.

lim Chinese have trained in these camps and returned to Xinjiang to carry out terrorism against the Chinese government. By working with the United States, China hoped to further its own campaign to stamp out terrorism within its own borders.

Human Rights

At the root of the differences between China and the United States (and many other Western powers) is their different views about the meaning of human rights. American and European traditions guarantee individuals extensive freedoms, even at the expense of group unity. In contrast, the Chinese have valued just the opposite throughout their history. The individual must generally yield to group values, according to Confucian teaching. Human relations are linked to a complex chain of authority figures in which each person owes obedience to someone higher on the chain: children to parents, wife to husband, youth to elders, subjects to those in authority. In a Confucian society, the government's major obligation is less focused on guaranteeing individual rights and more on providing the conditions for adequate food and safe shelter.

China specialist Francesco Sisci points out, in fact, that the Chinese words for human rights are actually Japanese interpretations of the Western idea of human rights, and that this concept was exported to China in the early twentieth century. Sisci writes,

> The lack of an indigenous word for "rights" in the Chinese language stems largely from the nature of the traditional social relationship between the individual and the state. Whereas in Western thought, government is instituted for the purpose of protecting man's inalienable or "natural" rights to life, liberty and property, for the Chinese, whose conceptions are profoundly influenced by Confucian thought as well as Mao Zedong Thought, such a notion is to some extent incredible. . . . There is no word bearing any resemblance to the Western concept of "rights."[83]

Freedom of Religion

The United States also censures China's government for repressing religious freedom. Although the Chinese constitution guarantees religious freedom, all religious groups must be authorized by the Religious Affairs Bureau of the State Council. For the Chinese government, the basic issue is whether clerics cooperate with the government. If they appear to have any political aspirations they will be suppressed for activities that "disrupt public order, impair the health of citizens or interfere with the educational system of the state."[84] This broad statement is easily applied to groups such as Falun Gong, which publicly demonstrates against government control and calls on its followers to avoid modern medical aid.

Today the government recognizes five official religions: Buddhism, by far the largest with 100 million or more practicing followers; Taoism, with no official count (many people combine Buddhism with Taoism); Islam, with 18 to 20 million; Protestantism, with about 10 million; and the Catholic Patriotic Association, with over 4 million. Those who want to avoid government approved religious institutions must practice in secret. As a result, there are sometimes both officially sanctioned and underground groups with similar religious beliefs practicing in China. The Religious Affairs Bureau occasionally detains and interrogates the clerics of these underground faiths. However, if the worshipers do not engage in political activities and only worship in private, the government usually leaves them alone.

Tibet

Another sticking point in Chinese and U.S. relations is Tibet, over which China has long claimed sovereignty. Although the United States tends to argue that Tibet should be independent, Chinese authorities argue that China and Tibet have a long history of relations. Tibetans often invaded Chinese territory, and China often imposed its will on Tibet. During the Tang dynasty, for example, Tibetan soldiers actually occupied the Chinese capital of Changan (modern-day Xi'an) in 763. In the early eighteenth century, the Qing dynasty emperor sent troops to take control of Tibet. Tibet remained nominally under Chinese control until the 1911 revolution that overthrew the Qing dynasty, after which Tibet asserted its independence. China once again occupied Tibet in 1951 and now claims Tibet as what it calls an "autonomous region."

In 1997 President Jiang Zemin made clear the Chinese position toward Tibet in an interview on the PBS program *News Hour*, in which he claimed that China had suppressed a 1959 Tibetan uprising in order to reform a feudal society. He said, "In China, in 1959, we began to work to abolish serfdom in Tibet. And actually [theocracies] have been opposed by people throughout the world ever since the Renaissance period. And, therefore, what we did there was also that we worked to abolish theocracy in Tibet."[85] Chinese officials have made it clear

China's Provinces

that China has no intention of relinquishing territory that it has traditionally considered part of its borderland.

The World Trade Organization

China's future relations with the world and its own internal reform process are now intertwined with its membership in the World Trade Organization (WTO). All economists believe that joining the WTO will speed up China's reform—both economically and politically. In order to encourage foreign businesses to open up and expand, economists say, China must transform its own business culture to meet international standards of fairness and legal protection. In the competitive world of private enterprises, only the most efficient businesses will survive. International business experts say that everything from accounting procedures to labor conditions will need adjustment.

WTO membership will present some challenges to China. Because China must, as part of its agreement to join the WTO, lower tariffs, imported products will often be cheaper and higher quality than products made in China. The resulting competition will likely drive some Chinese manufacturers out of business and accelerate unemployment in some of China's cities in the process. In addition, millions of farmers will be unable to compete against some imported agricultural products, so many will migrate to cities to look for work. WTO membership "is a historic juncture," according to Yu Shen, president of the Shanghai Customs College and one of China's top WTO experts. "It's an opportunity for China to establish itself as a major player in the global economic community. Once you enter the WTO, you enter the world stage, and you must play by the rules."[86]

Those who favor China's participation in the WTO say that future generations of Chinese will benefit greatly. For one thing, they will spend less on many consumer goods and supplies as Chinese companies are forced to compete for business with foreign corporations. People also will be able to choose from a wider variety of goods.

Not only do Chinese consumers stand to benefit from joining the global economy, but so do Chinese workers. China has

Huge corporations like Coca-Cola are now able to advertise in China.

been a favorite location for multinational corporations' investments since the 1980s. Today about four hundred of the top five hundred firms in the world operate in China and employ nearly 20 million people, or 20 percent of China's urban workers. China's State Information Center reports that in early 2001 "investors from more than 180 countries and regions had launched more than 370,000 foreign-funded enterprises in China, [and] the contractual foreign capital involved had exceeded $700 billion, and the actual use of foreign investment came to $363.6 billion."[87]

Foreign investment appears to be driving a technological boom in China, which already is among the world's top producers of high-tech products. In an area surrounding Beijing University, the district called Haidian is considered China's equivalent to Silicon Valley. Along the streets are dozens of companies making and selling sophisticated computers and peripherals. Internet cafés in the area are packed with young adults and students. Edward Zeng, owner of Sparkice Internet Café, says,

Bypassing Blocked Sites on the Internet

It is practically impossible for the Chinese government to screen the millions of websites available on the worldwide web. Blocking major world newspaper sites only inspires other news groups and individuals to carry the articles. In many cases, articles are syndicated to scores of other news sources, so it is virtually impossible to keep interested Chinese surfers from finding information.

In his article "The Great Firewall," A. Lim Neumann of the Committee to Protect Journalists (CPJ) writes about his experiences surfing the Internet in China:

> The *New York Times* site was blocked, but *Times* articles on China appeared on the unblocked *International Herald Tribune* site. Many dissident sites were blocked, but not all. The site for Human Rights in China, a U.S.-based dissident group, was not blocked. CPJ's site (www.cpj.org) was accessible, but Human Rights Watch (www.hrw.org) was blocked. *Time* magazine's site (www.time.com) was blocked, along with CNN.com. But the *Far Eastern Economic Review* site (www.feer.com) was not blocked, even though it often features blistering critiques of the Chinese government.
>
> And although the Falun Gong spiritual movement is officially classified as a social evil, information about the movement is readily available from a number of sites. CPJ was even able to download pictures of the Tiananmen Square massacre, although most Tiananmen-related dissident sites were blocked. "People frequently ask me, who decides what to block? Who is in charge of this?" [says] Guo Liang, a philosophy professor and Internet expert at the prestigious Chinese Academy of Social Sciences in Beijing. "I haven't the faintest idea. Nobody knows."

"It's not that technology is a part of China's future. Technology is China's future."[88]

The WTO and Political Reform

WTO membership is likely to foster reform of China's legal system as well. *Asia Times* reported that by the end of 2001,

> the State Council, or cabinet, has tackled 2,300 laws and regulations. Some 830 of these were earmarked to be thrown out entirely. . . . The State Development Planning Commission has reportedly scrapped 124 regulations incompatible with WTO membership. The State Economic and Trade Commission has abolished 13 rules. The central bank has thrown out six. . . . Cabinet departments must still scrap or revise 1,000 administrative codes.[89]

Whether joining the WTO will also motivate further political reform is still an open question. The idea of political reform, although always on the agenda, frightens CCP officials. Chinese leaders intend to retain control over their nation's development, and they have demonstrated their determination to clamp down on any serious threat to social order or national unity. But most China specialists believe that any failure of the party to push ahead with political reforms will impede economic growth.

To a large extent, China's eventual transition away from domination by the CCP is already underway. Many observers believe that Chinese society will be led not by the sons and daughters of party members but by children of "technocrats" and businesspeople. They are growing up without the heavy political indoctrination of the Mao years. With opinions molded by Western ideas, they will work comfortably with people from around the globe. As the twenty-first century advances, China shows every sign of becoming a superpower in every sense of the word.

Notes

Introduction: A Long Journey

1. United Nations Development Programme, "UNDP Human Development Report 2001 Launched in China," July 7, 2001. www.unchina.org.

Chapter One: Mao Zedong Unifies the Middle Kingdom

2. Frederic Wakeman Jr., *The Fall of Imperial China*. New York: Free, 1975, p. 213.
3. Ross Terrill, *Mao: A Biography*. New York: Touchstone, 1993, p. 97.
4. Terrill, *Mao*, p. 104.
5. Terrill, *Mao*, p. 105.
6. Immanuel C.Y. Hsu, *The Rise of Modern China*, 2nd ed. New York: Oxford University Press, 1975, p. 687.
7. Terrill, *Mao*, p. 149.
8. Quoted in Edgar Snow, *Red Star over China*, rev. ed. New York: Grove, 1968, p. 173.
9. Theodore H. White and Annalee Jacoby, *Thunder Out of China*. New York: William Sloane Associates, 1961, p. 203.
10. Quoted in Snow, *Red Star over China*, p. 174.
11. Quoted in Terrill, *Mao*, pp. 192–93.
12. Quoted in Terrill, *Mao*, p. 194.
13. Quoted in Harrison E. Salisbury, *The New Emperors: China in the Era of Mao and Deng*. Boston: Little, Brown, 1992, p. 54.

Chapter Two: The People's Republic of China and Mao's Legacy

14. O. Edmund Clubb, *Twentieth Century China*. New York: Columbia University Press, 1967, p. 318.
15. Salisbury, *The New Emperors*, p.127.
16. John King Fairbank, *China: A New History*. Cambridge, MA: Belknap, 1992, p. 349.
17. Jasper Becker, *Hungry Ghosts: Mao's Secret Famine*. New York: Henry Holt, 1996, p. 53.
18. Quoted in Godwin C. Chu and Yanan Ju, *Great Wall in Ruins: Communication and Cultural Change in China*. Albany: State University of New York Press, 1993, p. 277.
19. Quoted in Uli Franz, *Deng Xiaoping*, trans. Tom Artin. Boston: Harcourt Brace Jovanovich, 1988, pp. 134–35.
20. Quoted in Maurice Meisner, *Mao's China and After: A History of the People's Republic*, 3rd ed. New York: Free, 1999, p. 281.
21. Quoted in Stanley Karnow, *Mao and China: From Revolution to Revolution*. New York: Viking, 1972, p. 174.
22. Quoted in Salisbury, *The New Emperors*, p. 234.
23. Quoted in Karnow, *Mao and China*, p. 199.
24. Quoted in Terrill, *Mao*, p. 346.
25. Quoted in Terrill, *Mao*, p. 349.
26. Quoted in Han Suyin, *Eldest Son: Zhou Enlai and the Making of Modern China, 1898–1976*. New York: Kodansha International, 1994, p. 381.
27. Quoted in Salisbury, *The New Emperors*, p. 331.

Chapter Three: Deng Xiaoping's Black-and-White Economic Cats

28. Quoted in Salisbury, *The New Emperors*, p. 208.
29. Ross Terrill, "The Mao Legacy: One Hundred Years Young?" *San Francisco Examiner*, November 14, 1993.

30. Quoted in Patrick E. Tyler, "Deng Xiaoping: A Political Wizard Who Put China on the Capitalist Road," *New York Times,* February 20, 1997. www.nytimes.com.

31. Quoted in Franz, *Deng Xiaoping*, p. 291.

32. Quoted in Tyler, "Deng Xiaoping."

33. Quoted in David Turnley, Peter Turnley, and Melinda Liu, *Beijing Spring*. New York: Stewart, Tabori & Chang, 1989, p. 27.

34. Quoted in Orville Schell, *Mandate of Heaven*. New York: Touchstone Book, Simon and Schuster, 1994, pp. 58–59.

35. Quoted in Donald Morrison, ed., *Massacre in Beijing: China's Struggle for Democracy*. New York: Time Inc. Books, 1989, p. 144.

36. Quoted in Schell, *Mandate of Heaven*, p. 245.

37. Francesco Sisci, "Part 1: The Dream of Stability: Chapter 1: Fun for the Masses. 1.4 An Unstable Stability," *Asia Times*, March 17, 2001. http://atimes.com.

38. Todd Crowell and Thomas Hon Wing Polin, "Asian of the Century: Politics and Government, Deng Xiaoping," *Asiaweek*, 1999. http://cnn.com.

Chapter Four: Jiang Zemin and Party Reform

39. C.H. Kwan, "The Role of the Chinese Communist Party Coming to an End," *Voice*, July 2000. www.brook.edu.

40. Andy Xie, "Past Reforms Leave System in Line for Shake-Up," *South China Morning Post*, January 14, 1999. http://special.scmp.com.

41. Andy Kennedy, "The Tighter China's Grip, the Weaker the Hand," *Washington Post National Weekly Edition*, January 25, 1999, p. 23.

42. Sisci, "Part 1: The Dream of Stability: Chapter 1."

43. Quoted in Willy Wo-Lap Lam, "Bitter Harvest May Await China's Leaders," CNN.com, January 24, 2001. http://asia.cnn.com.

44. Terry McCarthy, "Lost Generation," *Time Asia*, October 23, 2000. www.time.com.

45. Jaime A. Florcruz, "China's Crisis of Faith," *Time Asia*, November 2, 1999. www.time.com.

46. Willy Wo-Lap Lam, "Can China's Communist Party Stay in the Driving Seat?" CNN.com, March 14, 2001. http://asia.cnn.com.

47. Yan Shuhan, interview by Allen T. Cheng, "Shades of Red: A New Chinese Ideologist Reveals Conflicts Within the Party and the Struggle to Tame the Old Marxists Opposed to Jiang Zemin's Reforms," *Asiaweek*, September 7, 2001. www.asiaweek.com.

48. Quoted in Xinhua News Agency, "Jiang Zemin on Theoretical Innovation," August 31, 2001.

49. Quoted in U.S. Embassy, Beijing, "China's Top Worries: Lagging Political Reform, Corruption, Environment," Environment, Science, and Technology Report, May 2000. www.usembassy-china.org.

50. Zhang Li-Fen, "China's Private Lives," BBC News Online, September 29, 1999. http://news.bbc.co.uk.

51. Human Rights Watch, "Nipped in the Bud: The Suppression of the China Democracy Party," September 2000. www.hrw.org.

52. Quoted in A. Lim Neumann, "The Great Firewall," *CPJ Briefings: Press Freedom Reports from Around the World*, January 1, 2001. www.cpj.org.

53. Quoted in Committee to Protect Journalists, "China," 2000. www.cpj.org.

54. *People's Daily*, "Constitution of the People's Republic of China." http://english.peopledaily.com.

55. Bureau of Democracy, Human Rights, and Labor, "China: Country Reports on Human Rights Practices—2000," U.S. Department of State, February 2001. www.state.gov.

56. Pei Minxin, "Cracked China," *Foreign Policy*, September/October 2001. www.foreignpolicy.com.

57. Howard Goldblatt, "Pushing the (Red) Envelope," *Time Asia*, October 23, 2000. www.time.com.

58. *Time Asia*, "The Pen Is Nastier than the Sword," October 23, 2000. www.time.com.

59. Quoted in Arnold Zeitlin, "Is the Stranglehold Easing? China's Party Daily Advocates 'Right of Being Informed,'" Freedom Forum, September 10, 2001. www.freedomforum.org.

60. Allison Liu Jernow, "China: The Tight Leash Loosens," *Columbia Journalism Review*, January/February 1994. www.cjr.org.

61. Quoted in Neumann, "The Great Firewall."

62. Quoted in Neumann, "The Great Firewall."

63. Quoted in Neumann, "The Great Firewall."

64. Anne F. Thurston, "Muddling Toward Democracy: Political Change in Grassroots China," *Peaceworks*, August 1998.

65. Quoted in Kevin Platt, "China's Village Elections Hint at Democracy," *Christian Science Monitor*, March 26, 1997. www.csmonitor.com.

66. Zhao Suisheng, "Liberalization in China and the Prospects for Democracy," CNN.com, 1999. http://cnn.co.uk.

Chapter Five: China's Future: The New Generation

67. Quoted in Crowell and Polin, "Asian of the Century."

68. McCarthy, "Lost Generation."

69. Lisa Movius, "To Be Young, Chinese, and Weiku," *Salon*, May 30, 2001. www.salon.com.
70. Quoted in Movius, "To Be Young, Chinese, and Weiku."
71. Movius, "To Be Young, Chinese, and Weiku."
72. Chu and Ju, *Great Wall in Ruins*, p. 271.
73. Chu and Ju, *Great Wall in Ruins*, p. 185.
74. Quoted in Louisa Lim, "China's Elderly Face Solitary Future," BBC News Online, January 3, 2002. http://news.bbc.co.uk.
75. Zhang Wei, "Relationships." www2.fli.cnu.edu.
76. Xia Meng, "Chinese Townspeople's Ideas on Marriage." www2.fli.cnu.edu.
77. BBC News Online, "China's Youth Wants Sexual Freedom," June 15, 1999. http://news.bbc.co.uk.
78. Yan Li, "China's Supreme Court Explains Marriage Laws," *People's Daily*, December 27, 2001. http://english.peopledaily.com.
79. Geremie R. Barme, "Big Think: Intellectionalism Did Not Die with the 1980s," *Time Asia*, October 23, 2000. www.time.com.
80. Quoted in *Toronto Star*, "Mao Leaves Today's Leaders in His Wake," July 30, 2001.
81. Zhang, "China's Private Lives."
82. Hannah Beech, "Bringing the Best and Brightest Back Home," *Time Asia*, October 23, 2000. www.time.com.
83. Francesco Sisci, "Part 1: The Dream of Stability: Chapter 3: Inhuman Rights? 3.2 Representing Human Rights," *Asia Times*, March 31, 2001. http://atimes.com.
84. "Constitution of the People's Republic of China," *People's Daily* Chapter II, Article 36. http://english.peopledaily. com.
85. Jiang Zemin, interview by Jim Lehrer, *News Hour*, October 30, 1997. www.pbs.org.

86. Quoted in Dorinda Elliott, "Playing by the Rules," *Asiaweek*, December 7, 2001. www.pathfinder.com.

87. *Asia Times*, "Foreign Firms Flock In," December 13, 2001. http://atimes.com.

88. Quoted in Joshua Cooper Ramo, "Haidian District: China's Silicon Valley, 1999: Where a Nation Plots Its Hardwired Future," *Time Asia*, September 27, 1999. www.time.com.

89. *Asia Times*, "Rush to Deregulate Continues," December 13, 2001. http://atimes.com.

Chronology

1911
The Qing dynasty is overthrown.

1912
The Republic of China is established.

1914
World War I begins.

1915
Japan issues its Twenty-one Demands.

1919
The Treaty of Versailles officially ends World War I. The May Fourth Movement emerges; students protest against the Treaty of Versailles.

1921
The Chinese Communist Party is founded in Beijing.

1925
Sun Yatsen dies; Chiang Kaishek becomes leader of the Guomindang (Nationalist Party).

1927
Chiang Kaishek launches a campaign to eliminate the Chinese Communists.

1934
The Long March occurs; Communists retreat six thousand miles to northern China.

1936
The Guomindang and the Communists form a temporary united front to fight the Japanese.

1937
Marco Polo Bridge incident ignites the War of Resistance Against Japanese Aggression, as World War II is known in China.

1945
World War II ends.

1946–1949
Civil war erupts between the Guomindang and the Communists.

1949
Communists declare the People's Republic of China under Mao Zedong's leadership; Chiang Kaishek and his supporters retreat to Taiwan.

1950
Agrarian reform, including extensive land redistribution to peasants, begins.

1950–1953
The Korean War occurs.

1953–1956
Collectivization of farms takes place.

1958–1960
The Great Leap Forward is instituted.

1960
A split between China and the Soviet Union develops.

1966
The Great Proletarian Cultural Revolution begins.

1969
To end the Cultural Revolution, Mao sends youth to the countryside to learn from the peasants.

1972
U.S. president Richard Nixon visits China.

1976
Zhou Enlai and Mao Zedong die; Deng Xiaoping returns to government; the Gang of Four is arrested.

1978
The CCP approves of Deng Xiaoping's economic reform program, including opening up to the West for trade.

1979
The United States and the PRC establish diplomatic relations.

1980
China's economy begins a five-year, record-breaking expansion.

1981
Deng criticizes the Cultural Revolution and states that Mao made mistakes during his rule.

1986
Intellectuals and students call for political reform.

1989
The Tiananmen Square Democracy movement is suppressed by the PLA; Jiang Zemin is named secretary-general of the Central Committee of the CCP.

1993
The Eighth National Party Congress meets; Jiang Zemin is elected president of the PRC and chairman of the Central Military Commission.

1997
Deng Xiaoping dies; the Fifteenth National Party Congress of the CCP meets and reaffirms Jiang Zemin's leadership.

2001
China becomes a full member of the World Trade Organization.

For Further Reading

Books

John King Fairbank, *China: A New History*. Cambridge, MA: Belknap, 1992. An excellent overview of Chinese history. There is no better book to read for an understanding of China's place in world history and the cultural influences that have created modern China.

Donald Morrison, ed., *Massacre in Beijing: China's Struggle for Democracy*. New York: Time, 1989. There are many good books that cover the spring 1989 demonstrations in Tiananmen Square. This is an excellent collection of articles by *Time* correspondents who were on the scene. It includes a time line from President Nixon's 1972 visit to China, with more details on the democracy movement between 1986 and the summer of 1989. It also has glossaries with a "Who's Who in China" and a list of common Chinese terms.

Harrison E. Salisbury, *The New Emperors: China in the Era of Mao and Deng*. Boston: Little, Brown, 1992. This is a penetrating look at Mao's and Deng's careers, especially after the formation of the PRC. There are disturbing revelations about the deaths of Li Shaoqi, Lin Biao, and other loyal members of the party who worked closely with Mao.

Ross Terrill, *Mao: A Biography*. New York: Touchstone, 1993. One of the classic biographies—well written and authoritative. It also provides the reader with an outstanding introduction to Chinese history during Mao's lifetime.

Websites

Beijing Scene (www.beijingscene.com). *Beijing Scene* is advertised as "China's Best Bilingual Lifestyle Magazine." It does cover this well, but it is light on politics. A recent issue included a profile of novelist Zhang Jie, an article on the meanings of colors in China, classifieds, columns on pop music, and trendy places to eat.

"China: Fifty Years of Communism" (http://news.bbc.co.uk). This BBC News special report gives an excellent review of the PRC. It includes analyses of the economy, foreign affairs, Cultural Revolution, the challenge of cyberspace, Jiang Zemin's position as leader, and other topics. It also has audio and video to accompany some stories.

Muzi China (http://china.muzi.com). This comprehensive site covers all aspects of Chinese life, including aspects of daily life, youth news, politics, entertainment, literature, and business. It also offers polls on Chinese popular culture and politics and chat rooms.

People's Daily (http://english.peopledaily.com). This is the website of the official Communist Party–sponsored newspaper. It details the daily activities in the country and also offers articles on the government and party structure, profiles of leaders, a copy of the Chinese constitution, and the published papers of Deng Xiaoping, among other material.

Shanghai-Star (www.chinadaily.com). This thorough weekly Chinese newsmagazine includes sections on world and national news, sports, business, lifestyle, fashion, people, travel, culture, and opinion.

"Visions of China: Fifty and Beyond" (http://cnn.co.uk). This outstanding CNN special reviews the fifty years since Mao declared the PRC. It includes contrasting views on social and political issues, a projection of China fifty years ahead, profiles of up-and-coming leaders, and video links.

Works Consulted

Books

Jasper Becker, *Hungry Ghosts: Mao's Secret Famine*. New York: Henry Holt, 1996. This is a detailed account of the extensive famine that resulted from Mao Zedong's Great Leap Forward program of the late 1950s. It includes details of the deceit and incompetence of officials.

Godwin C. Chu and Yanan Ju, *Great Wall in Ruins: Communication and Cultural Change in China*. Albany: State University of New York Press, 1993. This is an excellent account of how much the Chinese have changed since 1980 in their social and cultural views.

O. Edmund Clubb, *Twentieth Century China*. New York: Columbia University Press, 1967. The last U.S. consul general in Beijing before the Communists took over in 1949, Clubb's account of China is essentially a political history from the Qing dynasty, through Chiang Kaishek's failed attempts to rally all Chinese behind his leadership, to the flawed attempts of the Communists to establish China as a major world power.

Uli Franz, *Deng Xiaoping*. Trans. Tom Artin. Boston: Harcourt Brace Jovanovich, 1988. Franz's biography is dated, published nine years before Deng's death and before the 1989 Tiananmen tragedy. The book offers a favorable account of Deng's long career as a leader of the Communist movement and his pragmatic approach for bringing China's economy into the modern age.

Immanuel C.Y. Hsu, *The Rise of Modern China.* 2nd ed. New York: Oxford University Press, 1975. This is a thorough coverage of China's history from the Qing dynasty to the early 1970s from the point of view of a Chinese historian. It has extensive coverage of social, intellectual, and political developments of the twentieth century.

Stanley Karnow, *Mao and China: From Revolution to Revolution.* New York: Viking, 1972. This is an extensive account of Mao Zedong's attempts to correct what he saw as a revolution gone astray by launching the Cultural Revolution during the 1960s.

Maurice Meisner, *Mao's China and After: A History of the People's Republic.* 3rd ed. New York: Free, 1999. An analysis of contemporary China, Meisner's study covers the economic and political details of the Mao and Deng era.

Orville Schell, *Mandate of Heaven.* New York: Touchstone Book, Simon and Schuster, 1994. Schell begins with his personal experiences and goes on to analyze the background and events of the 1989 Tiananmen demonstrations. He then describes the changes in Chinese society stimulated by Deng Xiaoping's economic revolution.

Edgar Snow, *Red Star over China.* Rev. ed. New York: Grove, 1968. This classic book introduced Mao Zedong and his colleagues to the Western world during the late 1930s. Snow's book offers extensive personal accounts by Mao of the Communist movement.

Han Suyin, *Eldest Son: Zhou Enlai and the Making of Modern China, 1898–1976.* New York: Kodansha International, 1994. This biography of China's best-loved leader covers Zhou's personality from youth through old age and his intense love of his country. Han's account is based on both research and firsthand friendship with Zhou Enlai. It includes an excellent appendix with biographical sketches of almost every person who was involved in Chinese politics during Zhou's lifetime.

David Turnley, Peter Turnley, and Melinda Liu, *Beijing Spring*. New York: Stewart Tabori & Chang, 1989. An outstanding collection of vivid photos, with an excellent summary by Liu of the events of spring, 1989 in Beijing.

Frederic Wakeman Jr., *The Fall of Imperial China*. New York: Free, 1975. Wakeman details the social and political conditions that led to the fall of imperial China and the rise of Sun Yatsen and the republican movement in China.

Theodore H. White and Annalee Jacoby, *Thunder Out of China*. New York: William Sloane Associates, 1961. This book consists of the authors' firsthand accounts of their extensive travel and interviews with both the Communists and Guomindang military forces during the 1940s. They describe the living conditions of the peasants, Chiang Kaishek's wartime government, and the reasons the Communists gained the peasants' support.

Periodicals

Andy Kennedy, "The Tighter China's Grip, the Weaker the Hand," *Washington Post National Weekly Edition*, January 25, 1999.

Ross Terrill, "The Mao Legacy: One Hundred Years Young?" *San Francisco Examiner*, November 14, 1993.

Anne F. Thurston, "Muddling Toward Democracy: Political Change in Grassroots China," *Peaceworks*, August 1998.

Toronto Star, "Mao Leaves Today's Leaders in His Wake," July 30, 2001.

Xinhua News Agency, "Jiang Zemin on Theoretical Innovation," August 31, 2001.

Internet Sources

Asia Times, "Foreign Firms Flock In," December 13, 2001. http://atimes.com.

——, "Rush to Deregulate Continues," December 13, 2001. http://atimes.com.

Geremie R. Barme, "Big Think: Intellectionalism Did Not Die with the 1980s," *Time Asia*, October 23, 2000. www.time.com.

BBC News Online, "China's Youth Wants Sexual Freedom," June 15, 1999. http://news.bbc.co.uk.

Hannah Beech, "Bringing the Best and Brightest Back Home," *Time Asia*, October 23, 2000. www.time.com.

Bureau of Democracy, Human Rights, and Labor, "China: Country Reports on Human Rights Practices—2000," U.S. Department of State, February 2001. www.state.gov.

CNN.com, "China Steps Up Pollution War," January 13, 2002. www.cnn.com.

Committee to Protect Journalists, "China," 2000. www.cpj.org.

——, "China: Government Issues New List of Banned Media Topics," August 10, 2001. www.cpj.org.

Todd Crowell and Thomas Hon Wing Polin, "Asian of the Century: Politics and Government, Deng Xiaoping," *Asiaweek*, 1999. http://cnn.com.

Deng Xiaoping, "Remarks on Successive Drafts of the 'Resolution on Certain Questions in the History of Our Party Since the Founding of the People's Republic of China,'" March 1980–June 1981. http://english.peopledaily.com.

Dorinda Elliott, "Playing by the Rules," *Asiaweek*, December 7, 2001. www.pathfinder.com.

Jaime A. Florcruz, "China's Crisis of Faith," *Time Asia*, November 2, 1999. www.time.com.

Forbes, "China's One Hundred Richest Business People: Complete List by Rank," November 11, 2001. www.forbes.com.

Howard Goldblatt, "Pushing the (Red) Envelope," *Time Asia*, October 23, 2000. www.time.com.

Human Rights Watch, "Nipped in the Bud: The Suppression of the China Democracy Party," September 2000. www.hrw.org.

Allison Liu Jernow, "China: The Tight Leash Loosens," *Columbia Journalism Review*, January/February 1994. www.cjr. org.

Jiang Zemin, interview by Jim Lehrer, *News Hour*, October 30, 1997. www.pbs.org.

Jeremy Kahn, "Fortune Global Five Hundred: The World's Largest Corporations," *Fortune*, July 23, 2001. www. fortune.com.

C.H. Kwan, "The Role of the Chinese Communist Party Coming to an End," *Voice*, July 2000. www.brook.edu.

David Lague, "Nonperforming Loans: A Finger in the Dike," *Far Eastern Economic Review*, vol. 164, no. 50, December 20, 2001. www.feer.com.

Willy Wo-Lap Lam, "Bitter Harvest May Await China's Leaders," CNN.com.

———, "Can China's Communist Party Stay in the Driving Seat?" CNN.com, March 14, 2001. http://asia.cnn.com.

Louisa Lim, "China's Elderly Face Solitary Future," BBC News Online, January 3, 2002. http://news.bbc.co.uk.

Terry McCarthy, "Lost Generation," *Time Asia*, October 23, 2000. www.time.com.

Lisa Movius, "To Be Young, Chinese, and Weiku," *Salon*, May 30, 2001. www.salon.com.

A. Lim Neumann, "The Great Firewall," *CPJ Briefings: Press Freedom Reports from Around the World*, January 1, 2001. www.cpj.org.

Pei Minxin, "Cracked China," *Foreign Policy*, September/October 2001. www.foreignpolicy.com.

People's Daily, "Chinese Prosecutors Uncover Seventeen Hundred Corrupt Officials," July 13, 2001. http://english.peopledaily.com.

——, "Constitution of the People's Republic of China." http://english.peopledaily.com.

Kevin Platt, "China's Village Elections Hint at Democracy," *Christian Science Monitor*, March 26, 1997. www.csmonitor.com.

Joshua Cooper Ramo, "Haidian District: China's Silicon Valley, 1999: Where a Nation Plots Its Hardwired Future," *Time Asia*, September 27, 1999. www.time.com.

Francesco Sisci, "Falungong: Part 2: A Rude Awakening," *Asia Times*, January 30, 2001. http://atimes.com.

——, "Part 1: The Dream of Stability: Chapter 1: Fun for the Masses. 1.4 An Unstable Stability," *Asia Times*, March 17, 2001. http://atimes.com.

——, "Part 1: The Dream of Stability: Chapter 3: Inhuman Rights? 3.2 Representing Human Rights," *Asia Times*, March 31, 2001. http://atimes.com.

Time Asia, "The Pen Is Nastier than the Sword," October 23, 2000. www.time.com.

Patrick E. Tyler, "Deng Xiaoping: A Political Wizard Who Put China on the Capitalist Road," *New York Times*, February 20, 1997. www.nytimes.com.

United Nations Development Programme, "UNDP Human Development Report 2001 Launched in China," July 7, 2001. www.unchina.org.

——, "Urban and Rural Pollution: Urban Air Pollution." www.unchina.org.

U.S. Embassy, Beijing, "China's Top Worries: Lagging Political Reform, Corruption, Environment," Environment, Science, and Technology Report, May 2000. www.usembassy-china.org.

Maria Christina Valdecanas, "From Machine Guns to Motorcycles," *China Business Review*, November/December 1995. www.churchward.com.

Xia Meng, "Chinese Townspeople's Ideas on Marriage." www2.fli.cnu.edu.

Andy Xie, "Past Reforms Leave System in Line for Shake-Up," *South China Morning Post*, January 14, 1999. http://special.scmp.com.

Yan Li, "China's Supreme Court Explains Marriage Laws," *People's Daily*, December 27, 2001. http://english.peopledaily.com.

Yan Shuhan, interview by Allen T. Cheng, "Shades of Red: A New Chinese Ideologist Reveals Conflicts Within the Party and the Struggle to Tame the Old Marxists Opposed to Jiang Zemin's Reforms," *Asiaweek*, September 7, 2001. www.asiaweek.com.

Arnold Zeitlin, "Is the Stranglehold Easing? China's Party Daily Advocates 'Right of Being Informed,'" Freedom Forum, September 10, 2001. www.freedomforum.org.

Zhang Li-Fen, "China's Private Lives," BBC News Online, September 29, 1999. http://news.bbc.co.uk.

Zhang Wei, "Relationships." www2.fli.cnu.edu.

Zhao Suisheng, "Liberalization in China and the Prospects for Democracy," CNN.com, 1999. http://cnn.co.uk.

Index

Picture Credits

Cover photo: © David & Peter Turnley/CORBIS
© AFP/CORBIS, 101
Associated Press, AP, 14, 28, 55, 63, 73, 78, 82, 83, 86, 96
© Bettmann/CORBIS, 31
© Bohemian Nomad Picturemakers/CORBIS, 57
© CORBIS, 26, 46
© Hulton Archive by Getty Images, 16, 19, 22, 24, 32, 35, 39, 41, 42, 47, 51
© Hulton-Deutsch Collection/CORBIS, 13
© Macduff Everton/CORBIS, 10
© Craig Lovel/CORBIS, 87
© Matthew Mendelsohn/CORBIS, 69
© Reuters NewMedia Inc./CORBIS, 59
© David & Peter Turnley/CORBIS, 61, 91
© Nik Wheeler/CORBIS, 89

About the Author

Tony Zurlo has taught in Nigeria with the Peace Corps and at a teacher's university in China. He lives in Arlington, Texas, with his wife, an artist and educator from China. His publications include the nonfiction books *Japan: Superpower of the Pacific*, *China: The Dragon Awakes*, and *Daily Life in Hong Kong*. Zurlo's poetry, fiction, reviews, and essays have appeared in over sixty literary magazines, newspapers, and anthologies.